So You Think This Looks Easy
Tales Of A Troubadour

JEFF HARRIS

KeyWestCowboy.com
ISBN: 978-1-09834-767-3

CONTENTS

FROM THE AUTHOR

Projects can be done alone, but sometimes it requires a team to get things done right. It is with my greatest gratitude of a few close friends who were part of my team to advise me and guide me through the completion of this project. Their input and hard work made this book available for all to enjoy. **A Million Thanks** to Norma Smith, Lynn Colosi, Pamela Smith, Harry and Jennifer Purdy, Temple Hancock and Lulu for helping me put this group of fun memories together.

Much Love,

Jeffrey

Forward

Who do you know that can get hundreds of people to sing, shamelessly, in unison, "I want to put my finger in your tushy hole. Try it, you might like it?" Yeah…you heard me right. And based on that perplexed look, devious smile or expression of sheer terror on your face right now…that's what I thought. Not a soul.

Well…I know of only one, and I am excited to share him with you through this uniquely entertaining (and might I add, true, series of short stories authored by my lifelong friend…the unencumbered, unabashed, inoffensively offensive, and appropriately inappropriate, Jeff Harris.

I met Jeff when he was eighteen years old and had already been honing his skills as a singer/songwriter for at least five of those years. How could I have known back then that twenty years later, Jeff, through his successful music career, would take me on an adventure through Copenhagen, Denmark, that I couldn't describe suitably if I tried. Nine days of bars, booze, bus rides, Christiania, pot, lesbian Eskimos, a broken toe, fresh bread and jam, and did I mention Christiania? In the bizarre world of my friend, these escapades are commonplace.

Anecdotes from this book will not only give you a glimpse of what life is like for a talented, mischievous and open-minded musician who has traveled through more than seventeen countries, performed thousands of shows in front of millions of people all over the globe, but it will also provide you with a respite from life that is often way too stressful and serious. So, sit back, relax, and enjoy the bobsled run…

It's a wild ride.

Author; LBC

Introduction

"I've traveled a lot of places, I've seen a lot of things in this life of mine. I'm wise for my age. A lot of first impressions, mistakes I've made a few, but there's just one thing in life that always remains true. When the sky is dark and there's nothing left to lose, when you're all alone and you're lost and so confused, when you're standing on the edge of life and thinking about jumping, when you're down to nothing, God's up to something."

Those are some of the words from one of my favorite songs I have ever written called "Up to Something." I have looked back on those words many times in my life and thought of them often during trying times to help me make it through. They still remain true today.

I've traveled all over the world. I've seen more places in my life with a guitar on my back than I ever dreamed a small boy from Pennsylvania would. Tromping all over the place most of the time alone. Meeting strangers and making friends along the way. I have spent most of my life around music, and my personal faith, family and friends have always helped me make it through. I've seen good times and bad times, rich and poor, beautiful and ugly, happy and sad and through it all I am still here. I have a lot of good memories, a couple of bad ones and a few regrets. However, mostly I have a lifetime of stories that I can share.

I never asked God to make me a singer/songwriter, it was a gift I was given and was smart enough to recognize early in life and work hard to refine my craft.

I am blessed with the things I have in my life - My family, my friends, my fans and my music. I am truly a LUCKY man, although at times it did not seem that way.

Here are a few stories and memories that I have on my amazing journey that can still continue. To quote singer/songwriter, Jamey Johnson, "You Should Have Seen it in Color."

The stories in this book are true because I was there to witness them. On occasion my memories were blurred, but to the best of my ability this is how I remember them.

Nobody Saw It But Me

Living a lot of my life on stage, I feel I have a pretty good track record of being the only one who sees some strange shit. Good and bad. Being a patron of an establishment with music, as an audience member most of the time, your attention is directed to the stage. The audience watches me. What they don't realize is, I watch all of them back. I have witnessed some of the strangest things you can imagine only from that viewpoint. Most of the time I see it all from MY vantage point. The problem lies there within. The ONLY one who saw it was YOU ALONE.

One of the things I love most about playing in a band is when you're on stage and something happens in the audience. There is a good chance some-one else saw it, too? You have witnesses. All with the same look - WTF? That *Holy Shit* moment in time. Most of my career I have witnessed it alone. Being a *solo* performer you are totally alone with an unrestricted view of everything. It can be mentally disturbing.

From that stage I have witnessed, fights, drunks, unimaginable behavior, sex, drugs and Rock and Roll. I have seen weapons, nudity, people passed out, carried out dead and alive. Some of the things I have witnessed left a scar.

In this book I will review some of those scars - moments in time that are burned into my brain as a memory. In the following pages, I hope to give you an inside look at me and why I am the way I am and do the things I do. What made Jeffrey. Remember some of the stories in this book I witnessed all by myself. I hope you enjoy them all.

Family

The best way to start this journey of memories is at the beginning. I was born Jeffrey Lee Smith March 22nd, 1970, in Bedford, Pennsylvania. Yes, my real last name is not *Harris,* it's Smith. I was born the third child and oldest son to my parents, Jerry Lee Smith and Patricia Hershberger.

I grew up in a simple middle-class American town called Hollidaysburg in the middle of the central Pennsylvania mountains.

Both of my parents were born and raised in Bedford, Pennsylvania. They went to school together and met at the age of fifteen. My father was raised on a farm just south of Bedford in Mile Level. He was the oldest son to Francis "Star" and Virgie Smith. The Smiths were a hard-working blue-collar family. My grandfather Star ran a backhoe and my grandmother Virgie worked in the kitchen at a local nursing home. My dad and his younger brother, Jim, grew up with jobs to do around the house and on the little farm. Dad would have to get up in the morning, feed the animals, wake Jim for school, feed and dress him and then walk with him three miles to catch the bus to school. My dad never made it to school on Mondays, because after he dropped off Jim he would return to the house because Monday was laundry day. Dad left home at the age of thirteen and went to work on a nearby farm. Dad said when he was old enough he went to work. It was an ethic he learned and instilled in me and my siblings very young.

Mom grew up a few miles north of Bedford in the little village of Wolfsburg, the daughter of Thomas and Mary Louise Hershberger. She had an older brother Don, and she was the young daughter in the standard post-World War II family. Mom grew up in a white house with a picket fence with a Dad, Mom, Son, Daughter and family dog, the picture of America. My grandfather Tom was an electrician for the State of Pennsylvania and my grandmother Mary worked for the local doctor who delivered me. They went to church, belonged to the local Elks club, played golf and Bridge, and attended cocktail mixers and Saturday night dances. My mom grew up in a house built by her grandparents on a nice piece of land and it was well manicured. She was a high school majorette, in the band and among the more upper middle-class social scene. Mom grew up in a more "comfortable" environment than Dad.

My parents met, at the age of fifteen, one afternoon when my father was helping my grandfather Star dig a ditch for a waterline. Mom was visiting at one of her girlfriend's homes and Dad walked over to talk to them. It was that simple, the moment my parents met and began to date. They stayed together until my father passed away in 1999.

At the age of sixteen, while still in high school, my mom became pregnant. Mom and Dad were married in Cumberland, Maryland on May 7th, 1958. Dad was seventeen and mom was sixteen. They had to get married in Maryland because at that time they were too young to be married in Pennsylvania. Dad moved in with Mom at her parents' house and continued to go to high school and worked. My mom quit school after eleventh grade and began to prepare as a new mother.

In 1959 along came Pamela Sue, followed by Cindy Lou, Jeffrey Lee and finally my younger brother, Troy Lee. Mom and Dad began an unexpected family and marriage very young. All of us children were unplanned and later gained nicknames. Cindy was *Quits,* I was *Slips* and Troy was *AH, Shit.* There is an average of about five years between all children.

In 1968 my parents bought their first house in the little town of Hollidaysburg, Pennsylvania, about thirty minutes away from Bedford and my grandparents. A little white three-bedroom ranch house in Hollidaysburg is where I grew up with lots of neighbors and loads of kids playing outside.

We settled into our little family life and all had a part to play. Dad took a job working at a local furniture store and worked days while Mom was a stay at home mom with the kids. They owned a home, so there were always chores to be done around the house. Grass to be cut, bushes to be trimmed, leaves to rake, wood to stack, garbage to be taken out and so forth. We all had our jobs. Later if we were old enough to get a part-time job, you did, but you still had your jobs at home. I always say *my father had children for three reasons. To cut grass, rake leaves and shovel snow.* After all us kids moved out of the house, Dad bought a big-ass riding lawnmower with a bagger and a snow blower. He had a plan all along. We were just free labor like the Amish, but we had food on the table, a place to sleep and were warm. Everything was taken care of.

My parents helped with their jobs around the home as well. I worked a lot with my dad and my grandfathers and they taught me a lot about tools and how to fix things. Guy Stuff. I learned about how to fix almost anything and this was before the time when we had the convenience of stores like Home Depot, Lowes and Walmart. You had to fix things with what you had available. A whole lot of creative *Redneck engineering* went on. "It may not be pretty, but it works," was said a lot. I learned lessons and information starting very young. Sometimes you have to think out of the box to get things to work. I grew up exercising my young mind to figuring things out, how they worked and how to fix them. I learned first-hand, use your time wisely, work smarter, not harder, have the right tools for the job and be safe. Still the most important underlying theme, *Get to work!*

We worked our whole life as a family. Dad started his own Insurance Agency and sold Real Estate later on. Mom eventually went back to night school. She got her GED the same year my younger brother Troy graduated. She said, "I quit with the first and finished with the last." Mom took a job at a local Elementary Cafeteria and she loved that job and the kids that went through that school. Growing up, each year we went from schools to sports, to holidays, to grandparents' visits, birthdays and family vacations. We were a normal hard-working, middle-class, Sunday church - going American family. We were raised right, taught respect and good moral values. We kids grew up and went off to college and began our own lives. Deeply instilled in us was the most underlying theme, *Get to work!*

It's also important to know, no one else in my family played guitar and sang. My brother and sisters could only play a radio. We still have no idea where my *Gift* came from? Maybe the Mailman was a guitar player?

Elvis, The Beatles And Mom

For most of you this will come as a shock, but I, a lifelong musician and music fan, grew up in a home with little or no *Beatles* influence.

Four months after my birth, my oldest sister Pam was killed in an automobile accident. She was eleven years old when she died and my family was devastated. There was my dad and mom, my oldest sister Pam, my sister Cindy and Me, the baby boy, a typical American family until tragedy struck. I myself have no memory of my sister Pam at all. Just pictures and items around the house that belonged to her or involved her existence.

One of my most vivid images, still to this day is a photo taken of Pam, Cindy and me all together. Pam was holding baby me and the photo was taken by a professional photographer like Olan Mills. That picture has been on the shelf in my parents' home my whole life. Although I have no memory of Pam, I have been told that she adored me as her little baby brother. I grew up knowing I had a *Guardian Angel* watching over me and still do.

When I was too young to go to school, even kindergarten, I spent the whole day at home with my mom. My dad was working and my sister Cindy went to school. In my parents' Living Room we had a huge console stereo. Probably the biggest piece of furniture with the exception of the sofa. It was huge. Inside was a turntable, an AM/FM radio tuner and a place to store record albums. That stereo was a big part of my life growing up and my daily routine. It, along with the music, influenced me back then in ways I never could have imagined.

My parents had two places to store records in their home. One in the stereo and another piece of furniture just called *The Record Cabinet* which held albums and 45rpm's from my parents and sisters. There were some great records in there. Upon my discovery of the music available, I would find the first albums belonging to a band called *The Beatles*. My sister Pam was a HUGE *Beatles* fan. She lived through *Beatle Mania*, had their records, and loved their songs and handsome looks. She was a *Beatle Maniac*.

Being young and naive, I would put on one of *the Beatles* records on the turntable and begin to listen. Soon after that, my mom would enter the room and ask me to put on something else and she would be crying? I didn't understand. She would just ask me to put on a different record, not *The Beatles*. I was bringing up a horrible memory and had no idea. I would immediately change the record.

My parents and grandparents were all big music fans. I remember my grandparents on my Mom's side and their record collection as well. They had big 78rpm records of Big Bands and Orchestras. They had records like *Glen Miller and his Orchestra* and were fans of Laurence Welk. We watched that every Saturday evening. My mom and dad were music fans as well. They were teenagers before and during the discovery of Rock n' Roll. Mom was a fan of *the cute boys* like Pat Boone, but her record collection had more from one artist than anyone else, Elvis Presley. Yes, Mom was an Elvis fan. She was a teenager growing up during the discovery of Elvis and she was hooked. She saw his movies, bought the soundtracks and had a lot of his albums.

I remember learning very early during that time, that when she asked me to play something other than *The Beatles*, if I put on Elvis, Mom would sing and dance with me and stop crying. *The Beatles* were a cue to sadness, but "The King" made her happy again. Some of my earliest memories in life were there in that living room singing, dancing and laughing along with Mom to Elvis' music. I used to stand on the stoop step to our fireplace and sing and dance making Mom laugh as she played along. That was my first stage. It would remain my stage for many years to come.

I have always heard the phrase, "Music can either make you forget or remember everything." That's so true. The sound of *The Beatles* music brought back a tragic memory in my family's history and made my mother cry. I avoided *Beatles* music for years to come growing up. I still heard their music on the radio, but every time a song came on, Dad or Mom would change the station and never say a word.

Being a lifelong musician, it is very unusual to me that I grew up with no *Beatles* music as an influence on me. Elvis Presley's music, on the other hand, had a big influence. That probably is one of the reasons for my mild obsession with Elvis' music, life and history till this day. *The Beatles* played a huge part in a lot of musicians across the globe. They influenced future acts' music, style and dreams to write songs and become famous. Not me in this case. It's ironic that *The Beatles* were heavily influenced by Elvis and his music. Two of the biggest, most influential music acts in history. They influenced the World and generations to come. Strange how I grew up totally avoiding the one group at all cost.

In years to come, as an adult and a budding musician and songwriter, I did delve into *The Beatles* more: their music, their style and history, and I do play a few *Beatles* songs on stage now and then. I am a fan of the early years of *The Beatles* music like my sister Pam, but I don't much care for their later stuff and the Psychedelic era of music that followed. I am a fan of early Rock n' Roll.

In my world growing up, all I knew was *The Beatles* made my mom cry and Elvis made her smile and happy. There was no doubt on which direction I would choose every time.

The Purple Moose

I have always liked bars that had funny names. Maybe that's because some of my earliest childhood memories were snickering to myself during my family's one week summer vacation in Ocean City, Maryland. That was the first time I saw businesses with funny innuendos for names. I have always had a dirty sense of humor since I was a kid.

There were places like *The Brass Balls Saloon, Big Peckers Bar & Grill, The Bearded Clam and The Purple Moose*. I vividly remember walking down the boardwalk with my dad. I was probably only about five or six years old. We stood outside *The Purple Moose Saloon* and that was the first time I ever saw a live *troubadour*. I was hooked. I knew right then and there this is what I wanted to do for a living.

For those of you who are not familiar with the definition of the word *troubadour*: **Troubadour N. - a wandering singer or minstrel;** That is definitely what I do. I never heard that word used in the USA. In Europe they use that term commonly. The first time I was called that, a guy asked me what kind of musician I was? I answered *I am a solo act, guitar player, singer/songwriter*. He replied, "Oh, you're the *troubadour*?" I snapped back with, *You call me that again and I'm gonna kick your ass!* I was insulted.

The image in my head of a troubadour was the funny, little skinny guy in medieval times dancing around and playing ditties while wearing weird-looking, funny clothes. The man recognized my offense and explained to me that the job of being a troubadour is actually a nice thing. Respectfully meant.

The term *troubadour* goes back to the earliest of time. If *The King* wanted someone to sing and play for him, he would clap his hands and say, "Bring me the Troubadour." He wanted to hear music. If he wanted to laugh, The King would clap his hands and say, "Bring me the Court Jester." Same kind of gig. I figure there were probably a few troubadours around back then, but if you're playing for The King and you are on staff and on call, you must be pretty good!

He explained to me there were a lot of famous troubadours. Mozart, Beethoven and Bach were all considered to be *troubadours*. They *played solo*. Along with people like Bob Dylan, Paul Simon and many more. Don't forget Tiny Tim - "Tiptoe Thru the Tulips."

I figured if I can be in the same category as those guys? *Hell yeah, I'll take it.* OK let's face it, I am nowhere near as talented as those men, but I can "at least" claim I am in the same format as them. Technically. From that night on I proudly called myself a *troubadour*.

Meanwhile back at *The Purple Moose* (Waylon Jennings - *Dukes of Hazzard* Reference.) That night I stared at that troubadour singing and playing there on stage under the lights.

I remember liking the sound and there were people smiling, watching him. People were actually *happy*. I guess that is when I realized how music could move people. Little did I know I was at the beginning of a lifelong journey and love affair with music. For years to come, every time on vacation with my parents I would always stop outside the front of *The Purple Moose* and listen to whoever was playing on stage for a song or two.

I was too young to get in the bar, even though I was with my father, so we just stood outside watching and listening. I always wondered what it would be like to perform there on stage in front of that crowd? I always wondered if someday I would be able to do that? I held on to that thought for many years. The fact was I was young, I didn't play guitar till years later and I actually didn't think much about it when we were back home from vacation. Occasionally from time to time *The Purple Moose* crossed my mind.

After that, I always wondered what it would be like to play in Ocean City, Maryland. Many years later I found out. I was offered a gig and returned to Ocean City to play a place called *Fager's Island*. I finally answered the question. I played a few nights, then booked a different show the next day at a place up the road called *The Starboard* in Dewey Beach, Delaware. That is when I was introduced to a lot of new friends in the Rehoboth Beach/Dewey Beach scene. That is when I met a family I lovingly refer to as *The Delaware Mafia*.

I have been playing shows in Delaware every year for over fifteen years now in venues owned and run by *The Delaware Mafia.* I use that term as a joke. They are three brothers: Bryan, Spencer and Regan, with the Patriarch of the family, "The Don," "Big. D." He is a hard-working smart man. He has those boys in line and keeps everything under control. They ALL work hard. Big D. has taught them well. They take good care of me when I work for them, a lot better than some other places I have played in the past. There are good crowds at the shows and fun times every year when I return. I look forward to it.

Funny how I started with the eastern shore, went far away, and many years later, returned, only to be fifty miles away from the beginning. I found my destiny, answered my question and returned to a dream from long ago.

Although I never did play *The Purple Moose,* I have been back in there a time or two and had a beer. No one was on stage in the afternoon, everyone was on the beach. I bought a T-shirt and wore it on stage.

I started in Ocean City, Maryland and wound up performing in Rehoboth Beach, Delaware with a lot of cities and years in between. Things come full circle. I'm ok with that.

Two things I've learned,

1. You never know where life's road is going to take you?

2. I am convinced that *the court jester* and *troubadour* were the same person. If not, they were at least good friends.

Career Choices

When it comes to working, I have been doing it for most of my life. My father and grandfather taught my brother and sister and me a work ethic and responsibility that I still carry with me. Whether it is cutting grass, raking leaves, shoveling snow or doing your household chores, you've got to be responsible and do your part.

My first job was at the age of nine, I believe. I picked strawberries when I was on summer break from elementary school for five cents a quart, while most of my friends spent their summer vacations at the beach, swimming or playing baseball. I got up at 6 a.m., ate breakfast then my mom or dad would drop me off at the local strawberry fields to work till about noon.

A local family owned one of the most popular farm markets in the area and was renowned for their strawberries. The whole community looked forward to them and somebody had to pick them. Along with some other friends and strangers, I would crawl on hands and knees in those wet fields for hours, trying to mine those little nuggets of Red Gold. It was wet, miserable and hot after the sun came up. I would come home at the end of the day still a little wet, whether it be from the dew or sweat. I was stained and dirty and smelled like strawberries. All for five cents a quart that would be paid at the end of the summer. I didn't eat strawberries till many years later. After two years of that, I don't even think I made $100. It sure wasn't worth losing my sleep on summer break to get that wet and dirty. I could cut grass or do landscaping to make more money so I did.

At the age of twelve I started a job as a paperboy. According to the company rules I was supposed to be thirteen, but I think we lied about my birth date so I could get the paper route. Seven days a week, after school and on weekends, I would hop on my bike, skateboard or walk to deliver my forty-two papers to my customers. The route ended about three miles away from my house and then I would return home. Sometimes my parents would pick me up at the end of the route and drive me home if the weather was bad. I was making forty-two dollars a month, far more than strawberry picking, I was living like a king in my mind for a twelve-year-old. Like postal carriers: *Neither snow nor rain nor heat nor gloom of night stays these couriers from the swift completion of their appointed rounds.* Paperboys and girls are the same. I kept that route all the way through high school before I passed it on to my little brother. The paper route remained in my family for over thirty years until we finally gave it up. First me, then my brother, then my dad until he passed, and finally my mom until she retired. One hundred and fifty papers a day, seven days a week and by then it was 4 a.m. each morning, and we never missed a day. I am proud of that.

During my junior high school years I played sports. I played football, golf, baseball, was a pole vaulter and even wrestled for a year. Although I enjoyed playing sports, I was not the biggest, fastest or best guy on the team so when it came to high school sports I turned my attention to making money instead. Besides I wanted to buy a car and my paper route salary was just not going to be enough. I bought my first car when I was fifteen. My dad had to drive it home because I didn't even have a driver's license. I paid $335 for a 1966 Oldsmobile Cutlass 2 door hardtop Coupe and I still have it today.

While still working the paper route, I took a job at a local ice cream shop, *The Meadows.* It was a very popular place where at the time only boys could work. Some of my classmates already worked there and the local girls would come to see the boys and we would watch them too. Like social networking in the old days. I made enough money to buy my first car and with the income from the paper route I was doing alright. I thought about when it came time to graduate and go off to college.

I had watched my sister go off to college a few years earlier and I began to think about if I really wanted to go? So many of my friends were headed off in the fall and most of them had no idea what they wanted to become or do with their lives. It became clear to me that I had no idea what I would go to college for and I already had a job. I was making money, why do I need to go to college? I decided to take a few years and keep working to see what life brought.

Not long after graduation, I got a job offer to work for a local steakhouse chain for a lot more money than I was making at the ice cream shop and the paper route combined. There was a brief time when I delivered pizzas in the evening, but I was spending too much money on gas and wear-and-tear in my Hotrod.

I took the job at the steakhouse, began in the dish room and worked my way up to being kitchen manager and the head cook. I even got a spatula from them with my name engraved on it which I still use to grill today at home.

I was getting into what I call my *Randy Travis, Vern Gosdin and Hank Williams Jr. phase* of life. While all my friends were listening to classic rock and the beginnings of rap, I was discovering country music more and more and I loved it. All I wanted to be was like those guys on the radio. Working in the steakhouse was a dead end. I was going nowhere and I missed the outdoors, when I got a job offer to start working construction.

There was a brief period while working construction when I got my real estate license and tried to sell homes in the evening with my dad. I never sold a thing. Nobody wants to sign a thirty-year mortgage on the words of a nineteen-year-old kid in a three-piece suit with a red, hot sports car. That stint didn't last long and I understand why. It was back to construction full-time.

I spent about six months working for a friend who owned a seamless rain gutter business. He paid me a dollar more an hour than the steakhouse and I had weekends off, I was back out in the fresh air. I spent hours a day hanging off the edge of a roof and climbing ladders, sometimes multiple stories up, but I didn't care. I was making money, in great shape and had a good tan. I also began to take guitar lessons. I wrote some of my first songs hanging over the edge of a roof.

When winter came we could no longer work construction on the roofs so I was laid off from my gutter job. I took another construction job and did everything indoors from insulation, to drywall, to sweeping up to survive the winter. It was almost a year and a half since I graduated high school and I was thinking about college, but still had no idea what I would do?

In the late spring of that year, I was assigned to be the plumber's helper. If you don't know what that means, I can sum it up very easily. You are the guy digging the ditch by hand alone. Although I can't remember his name? the Head Plumber called me and everyone *Nit* - short for nitwit.

I would meet him at a build site of a brand-new house at 7 a.m. With just a brick foundation done, he would leave me with a pickaxe, a spade shovel, a rake, a string line and a level. He would make a mark on each side of the foundation and I was supposed to dig a straight ditch that went between the marks on a constant slope so he could come by and lay the main sewage line. All by hand! It was some of the best physical shape I have ever been in that summer oh, but it sucked!

Occasionally the boss would come back and check on me, but I spent most of the time alone digging a ditch. It was hot, sweaty and dirty that summer and I thought more and more about college. Later that summer I would arrive at the site about 5 a.m. at first light with my tools and radio. I would get to work to try and finish the ditch before the summer heat kicked in.

I constantly listened to the local country radio station and eventually became friends with some of the on-air personalities. I went to every country concert I could attend that summer and eventually the Program Director asked me if I wanted a part-time job running the Pittsburgh Pirates baseball games broadcast on the station? They were in the evenings and all I had to do was push a few buttons every once in a while, because it was broadcast by satellite. I took the job, I still dug ditches in the daytime, but then opened my door to the radio world and the country music I love so much.

One hot, sunny afternoon while digging, I was getting pretty tired and frustrated. The ground was tough and dry. I took a break and threw the pickaxe on top of my shoulder to catch my breath. Just then the pickaxe slid down the handle and knocked me straight on top of the head. I saw *cartoon stars* and stumbled for a moment before leaning against the foundation so I wouldn't fall down. I remember thinking *This sucks, you can't do this for the rest of your life. It's time to go to school, but for what?*

I remember seeing a commercial on TV about the Art Institute of Pittsburgh. They offered a Music/Video/Business program. They taught you how to work in radio, recording studios, TV, film, video production and in the music business. I already worked part-time at a radio station and I wanted to be Randy Travis, so this was for me. That fall I put down the pickaxe for the final time and headed west from my little hometown to the big city of Pittsburgh. It was time to go to college.

The Gambler

Many years ago one hot summer afternoon in Pennsylvania, I was working a construction job. I took a lunch break and stopped by a little convenience store near the site to grab something for myself. I was hot, sweaty, dirty and dressed in full construction clothes when I exited the store. As I left the curb a long, white Lincoln Town Car pulled up in front of me. It was shiny, clean and fancy - obviously a rental.

The driver rolled down the window and said, "Excuse me, do you live around here?" To which I replied *Yes*. He continued to ask me if I could tell him the fastest way to get to the Holiday Inn? From where we were at that convenience store they were way off path and were lost. I thought for a minute trying to figure out the easiest way for them to get to the hotel when the man in the passenger seat turned to me and said, "Kid can you tell us where to go or do I need to find somebody around here that knows what the hell they›re talking about?" It was Kenny Rogers!

I hadn't paid much attention to the guy in the passenger seat at first when they pulled up. I just noticed he was hiding his face with his hand and he had white hair and big diamond rings on his fingers. I ignored him until he rudely spoke to me. What he didn't know was that I worked for the radio station that was bringing him to town for his concert that night. We had promoted him and his music for weeks on the air and everyone was excited that "The Gambler" himself was coming to our little town. I was even going to go to the show myself, but now he was being a rude ass. I simply replied, *Oh, that Holiday Inn*.

I proceeded to tell his driver to continue down the road they were on for about two miles where they would come to a flashing light. Turn right down that narrow two-lane paved road and keep going. They would travel through fields and pass barns for miles and miles before coming to a giant intersection. The Holiday Inn they were looking for would be on the right hand side, can't miss it. I said *it will seem like you're going a long way but just keep going.* The driver said "thank you" and sped away.

I never went to the show that night and found out the next day that Kenny Rogers was such a prima-donna he refused to meet the radio contest winners backstage as we promised. He was just in a bad mood all night and the show wasn't that good. Maybe my fault? I didn't care. The next day the radio station pulled every one of his records out of the studio and never played them again.

I learned a very valuable lesson from Kenny that day. Be nice to people, you never know who you are talking to, and I remember that rule to this very day. I still don't like to play his music on stage, I only do it if it's requested. I will even turn the radio station if his music comes across the airwaves. I never forgot that day, he inadvertently taught me another lesson. If I ever need plastic surgery, pick a good doctor.

Playing For "The King"

During my early years of college in Pittsburgh, while I was working for a radio station, I was introduced to a guy named Scott who was an Elvis impersonator. Back in the early 90's at the Pittsburgh Penguins hockey games, he showed up at the home games dressed as Elvis. He got a lot of TV airtime for the stunt and the announcers started using the phrase "Elvis has left the building" whenever the Penguins were about to win a game. When there was no chance of the opposing team coming back, he would get up from his seat and exit the arena. A nice gig, and it got him his fifteen minutes of fame.

I became acquainted with Scott at some kind of radio function. We got to talking and I mentioned that I was a country music fan and aspiring country music musician. He mentioned he had a country band that played around town from time to time and invited me to come see them play at an area bar. I don't even think I was twenty-one when I went to see them play for the first time. They played a little restaurant bar where the stage was nonexistent. The restaurant just pushed a few tables away and cleared an area against the wall and the band set up on the same level as the people eating their prime rib. Not glamorous, but a gig.

During that evening he spotted me and we talked, then he invited me up to sing a song. All went well and I asked him if he minded the next time they played if I would bring my guitar along and just join in to jam with the band and he said sure.

They already had another rhythm guitar player in the band and when I showed up one night it caused obvious tension. In hindsight the guy was threatened by another rhythm guitar player in the band and thought I was out to take his gig. I really didn't care, I didn't want any money, I got to sing a song or two and all I wanted to do was play. It was only a few gigs until the other guitar player got fed up with the situation and quit. I took his place.

My sister Cindy bought me a new guitar amp with her credit card and said I could pay her back with the money I made playing. Little did she know most of the time I was playing for free.

For a few months I played with the band maybe once or twice a month at standard gigs: Moose Lodges, dive bars, birthday parties, community festivals, church events, restaurants and anywhere we could get a gig. Our niche to get the gig was, during the night at some point Scott, the lead singer, would slip into the bathroom and put on his Elvis outfit and we would do an Elvis set. That was it, our big claim to fame. I played backup guitar and sang harmonies for an Elvis impersonator. I didn't get paid, but it was fun.

One night I will never forget, we were playing at *The Route 88 Lounge* in the South Hills of Pittsburgh. It was a little dive bar in a strip mall alongside one of the usually traveled arteries that took people to and from their mundane jobs. The place was about fifty feet wide and fifty feet long, with a bar, a drop ceiling about seven feet high, a small stage in the corner and a usually irritated, hard-core alcoholic crowd who didn't care about music. I distinctly remember that room to this very day. There was a smog of smoke as you walked in. When you opened the door a cloud just washed out. The ceiling was stained yellow from all the smoke and the stage was so small we had to sit our amps on the floor. There was no room on the stage for all of us and the equipment. Scott, the lead singer, would have to stand on the floor off the stage because he was too tall and he would have to stoop over all night if he was on stage. It was classy – NOT! Either way a gig.

We had played there a few times and on this particular night the bar was full of people who had their backs turned to us, not interested in music or what we were doing. Somewhere in the middle of the evening a guy sitting at the middle of the bar slumped over with his head on the bar. There was some commotion between the bartender and patrons and there seemed to be some kind of medical problem. The bartender called 911 and the medics came to assess the man while the band took a break.

The medics took the man into the parking lot to assess him while the band stood outside trying to get some fresh air relief from the Marlboro smog. After a few minutes the guy said he was okay, refused medical treatment and went back inside. The ambulance drove away. We got back on stage and continued the show.

I can still see what happened next in my mind like it was yesterday. About twenty minutes after the ambulance left, in the middle of the next set, the guy slumped over at the bar again. The bartender again called 911 and the ambulance rushed back. They came into the room with a stretcher, put the man on it, covered his face with a sheet and wheeled him out. He was dead! The whole time the owner of the bar kept motioning to the band to keep going, keep playing, no one would notice. What? We're in a fifty foot by fifty-foot smoke-filled room with paramedics, a stretcher and a Deadman! No one would notice? Hell, you could hear the hand dryer from the ladies bathroom on stage and you think no one will notice this? They wheeled the man out in the middle of a song (I don't remember what song?) and he was gone. Literally gone! I remember thinking *Oh my God, we suck and we are so bad we just killed a man. We are horrible.*

That night on my way home I made a conscious decision to start my own band. The band was already getting more and more requests from the audience for me to sing more songs and Elvis was getting annoyed. I wasn't going to outshine The King. I knew it was time to talk to my college friend, Todd about starting a band. We had already jammed and written songs together, we had great Harmony, and it was time. I continued to work for Elvis for a month or so after that while secretly putting my own thing together on the side.

The last gig I played with the band, we had an audition to open for major country music stars at an Ohio music theme park. We traveled there on a tour bus owned by Earl Thomas Conley, which we borrowed because a friend happened to be his driver. We arrived in style like big shots. We did our audition and got the gig to open for Billy Ray Cyrus that year. We were so excited. This was about the time of *Achy Breaky Heart* and it was going to be a big opportunity for the band.

Not long after that, the band found out about my plans to start my own band and fired me. The original rhythm guitar player returned to the band and I was out. I never did open for Billy Ray Cyrus or play for Elvis again, but I think things turned out pretty well.

Young Dumb and Full Of Booze

On a fateful night in 1992 things with my band from college, *"2 of a Kynd"* came to a head. We had been doing very well regionally, playing clubs in Pennsylvania, Maryland, West Virginia and now Ohio. We were beginning to expand our reach farther away. We had been noticed by a national booking agent and we had just been booked a six-week run across the country. First time cross country tour.

We got a gig playing a place in Heath, Ohio called *Chubby's Country Palace*. Although the name sounded funny, it was a big club and a lot of national acts played there. It was the next step for us. We were playing a whole week instead of just weekends. The owner, Chubby Asher, was an older gentleman who had been around bars and music for years. Chubby was in his late sixties, very nice, with a lot of history and experience with bands passing through. He remarked that we were a really talented band, if we could just hold it together. He sensed there was turmoil within the band.

For the past few months there had been internal trouble. The band members Matt (lead guitar player), Mike (drummer) and Tom (bass player) had felt outcast over the recent band success and name. Although they were an integral part of the band sound and show, the band was focused on my partner Todd and me and our harmonies and songwriting. The band was called *2 of a Kynd* for a reason. The name was after Todd and me long before we added the other members. They were afraid they would be left in the dust if a record label had discovered us. We will never know. The other three members decided to call themselves *The Roadhouse Band*. Now it was *2 of a Kynd and The Roadhouse Band*, which drove even a bigger wedge between us and them. That's still a stupid band name.

We played a few nights of the gig and things were going well. Word was spreading around town about the young, hot guys in the band playing at *Chubby's* and the crowds were getting bigger.

On the second to last night after the show, I walked into the office to say goodnight to Chubby. The band had been drinking a lot of *Goldschlager* that night. It was our first experience with that liquor as it was just new on the market and not available in Pennsylvania. We indulged in it.

Upon entering the office, I discovered the bass player talking with Chubby and telling him that if he wanted to hire us again, he would have to up the price for the band. He was negotiating on behalf of the band without permission and the rest of us knowing. I was infuriated! No one speaks for me on behalf of my career but ME. They didn't back then and they don't today. I speak for myself and make my own decisions. I was still angry when we left the club and returned back to the hotel where the scene escalated.

In the hotel room I confronted the bass player about his actions on our behalf. I told him that he had no right. A few words were exchanged in the moment, enraged, I swung at him and went for his throat. I was prepared to smash the back of his head against the hotel room mirror. The rest of guys quickly broke it up and the argument continued. He verbally shot back at me with something to the effect of, "I am sick and tired of you thinking that you are 'the star of the show.' Anyone can do what you do. You're nothing special. Hell, I can do what you do. I can do it better." I said, *Fine, mother fucker, you're on tomorrow night.* I left and checked into another hotel.

I was tired of his drama and putting ideas into the heads of the other band members. The fact of the matter was he was the bass player. He couldn't do what my partner and I did. It was the magic of our two voices together that made the sound of the band, not the bass. I showed up the final night of the gig to fulfill my commitment to Chubby. The tension in the band was high and no one spoke to me. At the end of the night I said to the other members, *I am done.* I looked at the bass player and said, *If you think you can do what I do - good luck!* With those simple words, I left the band that I had started and worked so hard to build.

I cried all the way back to Pittsburgh alone in the van the next morning. It broke my heart that the rest of the band decided to side with the bass player - even my partner. But *it was what it was,* just another band break up story. In hindsight, I pissed away the most magical partners I have ever had. I have played with a lot of other musicians over the years, but still never had the same magical connection. It was truly a musical blessing and I pissed it all away over a bass player.

I returned home to The Band House in Pittsburgh, moved out within twenty-four hours and headed back east to live with my parents. I went back to working construction and my girlfriend was happy that I was not in the band anymore and did not have to go on the road. She never liked me being on the road anyway because of the threat of other girls and temptation.

I was working construction again, but I knew my musical career was not done. I continued writing songs and even wrote one called *I Don't Need You* inspired by the events of that night. I went back to the studio and recorded my second album. *I Am What I Am*. It was never released to the public, only to the music industry to no acclaim. It flopped.

I still missed playing with my partner, but there was a lot of damage done and we did not speak for many years after that night.

I continued to work my construction job and even had to take out a loan to pay the overdue utility bills they had stuck me with from The Band House. The bills were in my name, because I was the only one responsible enough to pay them. It was a very lonely, uncertain time in my life and I didn't know where I was headed next.

The only gratification I got was when I heard they hired another guy to take my place. Not the bass player. It was a childhood friend of my partner who was actually good, but he wasn't me. The band did do the cross country tour, but they lasted only two months before the band broke up for good.

In my heart I knew I had caused the breakup. Maybe a bad, rash decision? I also knew they could NOT do what I did and I tried to find my peace in that. It was hard. I was still uncertain of what my music and future had in store for me?

Many years later I am still here playing music and writing songs. The Silver Lining is, the last I heard, the bass player was working on a truck selling potato chips. Karma's a bitch!

Myrtle Beach

After the fall-out with the band I spent the next year working construction. I was hanging seamless rain gutter again with a friend through the spring and fall until winter came and we were shut down. I was still with my girlfriend, and her roommate's boyfriend had a snow removal business and he could use some extra help. I went to work with him much to my dismay. When I said he had a *snow removal business,* I mean he rode around in the heated truck with a plow while I was out in the cold with a snow shovel in my hand. We worked all night into the late morning and it was miserable, cold and wet. I still missed playing music and the band, but I was trying my best to just stay alive financially. I already had back problems and shoveling snow did not help. That winter Pennsylvania had record-breaking snowfalls and I felt like I shoveled every flake of it. As soon as I would get done with work, I would go home and get a hot shower and try to sleep. While I was sleeping the snow would start again and we proceeded all over again. I was miserable and it was starting to take a toll on my relationship with my girlfriend. When spring broke I went back to work in construction and our relationship came to an end. My girlfriend explained she was about to graduate in a year and needed to find herself and decide what she wanted to do with her life after college. In short, she dumped me. I don't blame her. I wouldn't have wanted to be with me either at that time. I was going nowhere and was just miserable because I wasn't playing music. I couldn't see it at the time but it was one of the best things that could have happened to me.

In the late spring while working construction I took a fall off a roof. I fell about twenty-five feet down and landed on my left hip. The only part of my body that came into contact with the house was my left hand. My left index finger caught the rain gutter on the way down and cut it almost off. I immediately went to the emergency room and they assessed my injuries. The doctor told me I needed to have x-rays of my hip and back. I also needed a CAT scan to see if I had any head damage. Finally, they would take a look at my hand. I told the doctor *I am a guitar player, I can play guitar in a wheelchair. I need you to take a look at my hand right now.* They immediately took me into surgery to repair my hand. I don't remember much before the surgery, but I do remember telling the doctor just before I went under *while we're in here let's put in a big fake set of titties while we're at it.* Then things went black. They reattached my finger back to its normal place, but told me the nerves had been cut and I would most likely never have feeling in that fingertip again. I was devastated. I was determined to play guitar again no matter what. It took me over two years to retrain that finger and get back to playing guitar again. For a while I played only four strings on a guitar until I could get that finger back to where it was usable. I had to play a nylon string guitar for a while because the pain of the steel strings was excruciating. Finally, I worked my way back to steel strings, first light gauge, then medium and then back to heavy, where I am today. Yes, I still play today, but have no feeling in my left index fingertip.

Late that summer, still not working due to my hand injury, I took a vacation to Myrtle Beach to visit with my cousins. I had found a country bar down there years before and really liked it and returned to watch the band. After a few beers I introduced myself to the manager and asked her if they were hiring? She replied, "Yeah we are looking for a head bartender, do you have any experience?" I replied, *Hell yeah, I have been tending bar for years and I would love to work here.* I lied. I had never tended bar in my life, but I was looking for a change. I had no romantic ties to Pennsylvania anymore, I couldn't work construction due to my healing hand, winter was coming fast and I wanted out of the cold. Two weeks later I had my Toyota Celica GT packed full of my belongings and headed south. I had no idea if this would work out or not? I knew no one other than my cousins who were going to let me stay with them. I was about to start a job I had never done before. I started in three days.

I cried most of the trip to Myrtle Beach that day. I was lost, uncertain about my musical career, my relationship with my ex-girlfriend and my future in general. In the back of my mind I knew that if things didn't work out I could always come back home to Mom and Dad's house, but I needed to make a life of my own. I arrived in Myrtle Beach and spent the next two weeks every day sitting on the beach and studying a bartender's book. I pulled it off and no one was the wiser. Thank God the bar I was working in was a honkytonk. Mostly beers, Beam and Coke, Lemon Drops and Tequila. Nothing fancy or I would have been screwed.

On my first night as a bartender just after we did last call someone came rushing back in through the front door and said call 911. Two girls who had just been in the bar left, got in their car and pulled out on the highway in front of a logging truck. The truck hit them at full speed and pushed the car about five hundred yards down the road into the trees before coming to a stop. I was terrified there was going to be some kind of big investigation about the accident and them being in the bar. I knew they had arrived late and I had sold them one drink each. They did not seem drunk to me. I felt bad about the accident, but I didn't want any trouble because I was new in town. There was never an investigation and I found out the next morning they were killed on impact. I felt bad and thought to myself *This is a tough way to start, I hope things get better than this.* The next night I went back hoping my second night as a bartender would be better.

Charlie's Nightlife

I can honestly say *Charlie's Nightlife* was a one-of-a-kind bar. A redneck, honky-tonk bar in Murrells Inlet, South Carolina just south of Myrtle Beach. The bar was owned by a singer/songwriter named Charlie Floyd. The best way I can describe it was every bit of the bar from the movie *Road House* without the chicken wire.

When I met Charlie he was at the height of his career. He had a record deal with Liberty Records in Nashville and he just had his first album released. His music was being produced by two of the biggest producers in Nashville, Jim Cotton and James Stroud. He was beginning to get airplay on the radio and things were going well. He was a mentor to me and I learned a lot from Charlie, some good and some bad. Charlie was a partier. He had a hot band, a rowdy popular bar and there were always guys, girls and temptations around. I saw a lot of it.

Although his career was doing fine, Charlie was dealing with a nasty blow he had recently taken in his career. While recording his latest album he had run across the song called *Achy Breaky Heart*. He wanted to record the song on his CD and considered changing it to Achin' Breakin' Heart because it sounded better. Upon a visit to *Charlie's Nightlife*, his producers saw him play the song live and told him he should cut it. When they returned to Nashville they also gave the song to Billy Ray Cyrus and as history speaks for itself after that, the song was huge. It was almost Charlie and not Billy. I am sure that weighed heavy on his mind as I saw him delve into the devil's ways more and more.

After about a year of bartending, Charlie used to call me on the stage to play a few songs alone while the band took a break. I played my songs until the band came back and then went back to tending bar. I was the *Singing*

Bartender. This pattern went on for a few more months until I no longer tended bar. I played with the band and sang when Charlie took a break or just didn't show up for the show that night.

I have so many stories about that bar and there is no way I can remember them all. Some because I was too drunk to remember and some because it's been so long. Here are a few I do recall vividly.

First of all, I don't like reptiles. I think they are gross. Every night before we opened or after we closed I found myself alone in the bar. There was a pond outside off the deck on the front. We had an alligator that lived in that pond and drunk patrons used to throw beer bottles at it for fun. We never had any trouble with the gator but the pond was full of beer bottles and frogs. Somehow or other? The frogs always seemed to get into the bar. Many times I would be working alone and hear something moving, it would catch my attention and most of the time it was a frog. However, this sight always scared the shit out of me. Not because I was afraid of the frog itself, but what it might do. Every time I saw a frog then and now, I am afraid the frog will turn to me and pull out a little top hat and cane and start dancing singing *hello my baby, hello my honey, hello my ragtime gal* just like Michigan J. Frog on the Bugs Bunny cartoon. No one would be around to see it but me. I know it sounds strange, but it still crosses my mind every time I see a frog. I am glad to say it never happened, because I remember how the guy in the cartoon went insane because of that stupid little frog.

In my first few weeks of working at his bar, I discovered Charlie's relation-ship of having a very *large family* in a small town. It seemed like EVERYONE who came in was Charlie's cousin and wanted a drink for free. Charlie lived in the Myrtle Beach area his whole life and it was hard to tell who was and who wasn't a cousin, niece, nephew, aunt or uncle. It never ended. One night during my first week bartending, I noticed a little old man walk through the back door and go behind the bar. He looked like an old Confederate soldier from a cartoon, small, gray haired, wrinkled and a little feeble but feisty. He poured himself a drink and I approached him. I *politely* said, *Who the fuck are you? You can't be back here and can't do that.* He brushed me off like he owned the place. I grabbed him by the belt and back of his shirt marching him towards the back door. Charlie approached me and said, "What are you doing?" I replied, *I just found this guy behind the bar stealing drinks and I'm about to throw his ass out of here.* Charlie looked at me and said, "That's my father-in-law." That night I met Charlie Patrick. He turned out to be a good man over the time I got to know him, just a feisty old bugger. I realized Charlie's family was everywhere and they just made themselves at home.

Another time, I busted one of Charlie's cousins shoving mini bottles of booze in the waistband of her stretch pants. She was a large woman and was already drunk. She put up a pretty good fight and cussed me out before we got the booze back and I threw her out. She was banned from the bar for a few weeks after that. She had half a dozen mini bottles stuffed in her pants.

Charlie had another cousin named Tommy. I don't know what was wrong with him. But he just wasn't right. Tommy did not have a license to drive a car, so he would ride to the bar on a big farm tractor with a bush-hog on the back. I would see him driving down the highway on that thing with the big orange triangle on the back and the cops couldn't do a thing to him. He liked to tie up traffic with it. Another one of his favorite things to do was get drunk, fire up the tractor and drop the bush hog on a beer can on the ground in the parking lot. He would rev up those blades and shoot that can across the parking lot like a hockey puck at a hundred miles per hour without warning. I don't remember anyone ever getting hit by a can. But I can only imagine the damage it did to some of those cars and trucks parked outside. He was nuts!

The bar had a plywood dance floor in front of the stage about 20' x 20'. At the height of Charlie's career, the dance floor was often packed. One night the band was playing the song *Jump* by Kris Kross. The whole band was jumping up and down on stage along with the audience on the dance floor. Suddenly the floor gave way and crashed to the ground. The band never stopped and the crowd kept going even though it had fallen thru several inches to the ground. It was a wooden building and the supports just gave way under the jumping. No one got hurt from what I remember. The crowd looked like a group of midgets still jumping up and down. Nowadays someone would have sued for that, (so sad) but back then it was just another fun night at the club and a great laugh.

The club had two floors. There was an upstairs U-shaped balcony that had a bar with chairs and sofas and a wooden railing that wrapped around, overlooking the dance floor and the band. Many nights I watched guys fucking girls from behind, bent over that railing while the band played along like a soundtrack to their porno. It was in full view of the band and everyone in the balcony, but no one seemed to care. Sometimes upon closing, as a bartender, I had to interrupt a couple in the middle of carnal pleasures on the sofa to tell them to take it to the parking lot. We were closing. It was just par for *Charlie's*.

One night for reasons unknown, the band started drinking tequila. We all took a break and headed out to the parking lot to sit at the picnic tables nearby. We exited through the back kitchen door and the audience went out through the main front door. While in the parking lot, I am not sure what happened. Someone threw a punch and the next thing I know the band and the customers were in a fistfight in the parking lot. In the midst of all the punches, kicks and yelling someone yelled, (maybe Charlie?) "Break's over." We all stopped, walked back into the bar and began to play again. The audience returned, started dancing and drinking. Everything went back to business as usual, like nothing ever happened.

One of the weird things about *Charlie's* was it was located in Georgetown County, South Carolina, just a few hundred feet south of the Horry County line where Myrtle Beach is located. The laws of each county were different. We had to shut down Charlie's at midnight on Saturday night because of the Georgetown County laws (no liquor sales on Sunday) but Horry County bars could serve until later. Every Saturday night with the bar packed we would yell, "Time to go". The whole bar, band and all, would exit the place, jump in their vehicles and drive up the road to the next bar across the county line and continue the party there. It was a weird thing, but it was the law and it happened every week.

One Saturday night, someone that I can't remember, showed up with a jar of moonshine. I had never had moonshine before, and standing in the back kitchen with the rest of the band we opened the Mason jar and began to pass it around. After a few minutes the jar was empty. I'm not really sure what happened after that. All I can say is I am pretty sure it was not a good show for the band. I woke up about a day and a half later at home, still fully clothed from the last time I left to go to work, boots and all. I walked to the window and saw my car sitting in the driveway. I still have no idea what happened that night or how I got home. It's all a blank in my mind. However, I did learn a valuable lesson: stay away from the moonshine.

Somewhere along my time in Myrtle Beach, Charlie decided to buy a tour bus. Not a regular customized tour bus, but an old Greyhound that he was customizing for the band and himself. It was New Year's Eve 1993 or 1994 I think. When we closed the bar after ringing in the New Year, a bunch of us boarded the bus and decided to continue the party on the road, crashing other New Year's Eve parties. The bus was not even close to being finished, but we went anyway. I remember plywood benches along the sides, maybe a bunk or two, and the rear master suite had an air mattress and a sleeping bag. At this point we didn't care as we all piled in and set out for parts unknown. And when I say parts unknown I really mean it! I still don't know where I was that night. All I remember is stopping at a house way out in the swamps and having a few drinks. A few of us sat around a picnic table drinking and smoking when we noticed the family for some reason had a six foot giant papier mache pig in their yard. WTF? Who has a giant papier mache pig in their yard? They did! We never asked about the pig before we jumped on the bus again. It was just strange. We wound up at a run-down motel somewhere and the party continued in someone's room for a few hours until we returned to the parking lot at Charlie's bar. I was drunk and lost on where I had been. They could have left me at either place and I would have had no idea which direction to walk to get home. We all exited the bus to our cars and headed our separate ways. I found out the next day that they drove the bus back to Charlie's house; they left it in the middle of the road and proceeded inside to have another drink and pass out. In the morning they found the bus was still in the middle of the road and running. No one ever said a word. Fun was had by all that night and no one got hurt, but I can still see that giant pig in my mind.

Speaking of pigs - the most frightening thing that ever happened to me at the bar was on a Labor Day weekend. I was tending bar at the time and I was still getting used to the *Southern* ways. I arrived early in the evening and began to set up for the night. I walked to the beer cooler we had out back and opened the door when I froze in horror. Lying on the floor of the cooler was something big wrapped in a bloody, white bed sheet. Amongst the blood and the cloth, I saw a bit of flesh-colored skin sticking out. I slammed the door in a hurry and stepped back to catch my breath. In my mind I thought, *Oh shit, something happened and Charlie killed someone and hid their body in the cooler. Now I have found the body, there's going to be police all over this place soon, they're going to be asking questions I don't know the answer to. Charlie is going to be in jail, there's going to be a long drawn-out trial and I'm going to be right in the middle of this. No! no! no! no! no! I don't want to be involved, but it's too late.*

I ran to the phone in the kitchen and called Charlie at home. I am pretty sure he could hear the sound of panic in my voice when I said, *Jesus Christ Charlie, what did you do?* He calmly replied, "What are you talking about?" I told him I had found the body in the cooler. He laughed and said, "That's not a body, that is a pig for the *pig pickin'* this weekend." I was still confused. Charlie was planning to throw a big *pig pickin'* at the bar. (That is a South Carolina way of saying a pig roast) and no one warned me about the pig being in the cooler. I hung up the phone, went back to the beer cooler, opened the door and peered in at the bloody sheet. I lifted one edge and a pig's hoof fell out. It scared me almost to death and I stumbled backward in fear. I slammed the door and did not go back into the beer cooler the rest of the night. That experience scared the shit out of me. Now I'm not saying Charlie is the kind of person to *kill someone*, but at the time there was a lot of partying going on and there was a chance that things had gotten a little out of hand at the wrong time. Luckily it was just a pig. I still hated opening the door to the beer cooler every time after that.

I learned a lot from Charlie over the years about how to be a better Entertainer, but the time had come for me to move west and give it a shot. I have seen Charlie a few times since then. He still performs around Myrtle Beach and Murrells Inlet. I have a lot of respect for him. He is truly a talented man who taught me tools that I still use on stage every night. If you're ever in Myrtle Beach, go see Charlie and tell him I said hello.

"The Killer"

I have seen a lot of legendary musical artists perform in my life. A few I remember at the top were Ray Charles, Conway Twitty, Garth Brooks, George Jones and a lot of *Grand Ole' Opry* stars. Hands down the best show I ever saw live was Prince. He holds the title with me as being the most talented Artist I have ever witnessed in concert. Not to mention I have never seen so many horny women in one place at one time as a Prince concert. The second best show I have ever witnessed was Jerry Lee Lewis for a completely different reason.

Somewhere around 1994 I witnessed Jerry Lee Lewis play his one and only show ever at *The Alabama Theater* in Myrtle Beach, South Carolina. The infamous "Killer" was coming to perform and I was excited to see him play live. I have always been a fan of Jerry Lee's music, but not his personal behavior in life. Let's face it, he is a crazy, bitter, old grumpy man, but he can play piano like no one else. I assume a lot of people have seen the movie *Great Balls of Fire*. That movie reveals some of the strange behavior of the man. Being a musician, I have heard for years rumblings of horror stories involving Jerry Lee and his behavior, his moods and difficulty to work with. On this particular night I was excited to witness the legend perform and nothing more.

I was seated in the front row of the balcony with a full view of the stage and a sold out crowd. The stage was set with a Baby Grand piano in the center, a drum kit, a keyboard and an amplifier for the lead guitar player and bass. A simple band set up and ready to rock and roll. The band walked out from the wings of the stage, plugged in and began to play. The grand piano was still empty, but the band just seemed to be jamming and faking their way through a song, setting sound levels. There was no opening act. The band was doing a simple sound check. That's when I realized that is exactly what was going on. They were walking out cold, unrehearsed and they WERE the opening act.

I took mental notes of the guitar player who was an older man, definitely in his sixties. He was wearing a red velvet smoking jacket and played an old baby blue Fender guitar. He looked totally out of place with the rest of the band who were much younger and dressed in black. I realized he was the *band leader* for Jerry Lee and he traveled to Myrtle Beach with him for the show. The rest of the players were just a *hired pick-up band*, employed to back up Jerry Lee just for that night. They normally did not perform with him and there has been no rehearsal. They were just winging it.

A few minutes into the sound check/opening act, in the middle of a song, a little, tiny man came marching out of the wings to the piano, walking like *Marvin The Martian* from the Bug's Bunny cartoons. He never said a word, he just waved his arm for the band to stop the song they were in the middle of then sat down on the piano bench. The band trailed off with a few remaining beats and notes on the abrupt ending, totally out of time.

Without a word, Jerry Lee immediately began pounding on the keys and started a song. The problem was, the band had no idea what song Jerry was going to play. There was no set list or game plan. He just winged it. The band would just pick up, playing along the best they could, trying to catch up and figure out what song he was playing. I thought to myself, *This is a nightmare for the band.* Even his guitar player/band leader had no idea what Jerry was going to play. Musical sacrifice.

Jerry would end each song with a little waive-down of his left hand from the keyboard, without a heads up. No cue at all to the band. The song just ended when Jerry Lee stopped unexpectedly and the band would try to clean up the ending with a *train wreck.* That's where the band all hits a note to accent the ending of a song. It was a nightmare to watch and I felt bad for the band. I hoped they were being paid well.

Somewhere in the middle of the first song or two, I noticed Jerry looking to the wings of the stage and pointing to his microphone, then to his monitor speaker next to him and then straight up in the air. This was a cue to the monitor man that he wanted to hear more of his voice in his monitor speaker. Monitor men are the ones who control the sound out of the speakers on stage for the musicians to hear. Each musician likes to have a different mix in their monitor. It makes the band more comfortable to perform when you can hear everything correctly. The monitor people are off in the wings so the audience cannot see them, but they are in direct line of sight to the band. They communicate through visual signals. Jerry Lee obviously wanted more of his voice in his monitor.

The monitor person turned up Jerry's voice, but it was still not loud enough for him and to his liking. He repeated the same signals to the monitor person again and again, each time becoming more and more infuriated. At one point he pointed to his monitor and gave the monitor person the finger in the middle of a song. When the song ended, Jerry said over the microphone loudly and rudely, "Hey you, monitor man, I told you already to turn this thing up. Get your shit together." Wow, he just cussed out the monitor man over the microphone. I thought to myself, *OK this is not really professional, but he is Jerry Lee Lewis and he has been known to be difficult.* Remember there was no sound check to get this stuff right before the performance. I'm sure the monitor person was embarrassed. Jerry did not look pleased.

Jerry Lee and the band played a dozen or more songs. Each new song unknown to the band, complete with a weird abrupt ending. He played a few classics like *"Whole Lotta Shakin' Goin' On,"* and *"Teenage Confidential,"* all to the crowd's approval, but he was still in a foul mood. I looked at my watch. The show had been going on for almost fifty minutes. I wondered how long of a show was he contracted to do? Probably an hour? Maybe an hour and a half? At fifty-five minutes he broke into *"Great Balls of Fire."*

The crowd went electric and rose to their feet as Jerry stood up and toppled the piano bench over backward. He was standing and playing with his feet, pounding the keys just like the movie. We all watched, clapped our hands, danced and sang along. What happened next was totally unexpected, but in true Jerry Lee style. As the song was ending, Jerry while still standing, kicked over his stage monitor. He proceeded to throw the piano bench on top of the Baby Grand piano, and then grabbed his microphone and turned to the band leader. Jerry yelled into the microphone, "**And for Christ sake Kenny, turn that God damn guitar down.**" He threw his microphone and the stand to the stage in a big crash then turned and stormed off the stage. He never said thank you, goodnight or a single word. The audience was in complete shock. They were upset by his outrageous behavior. I threw my hands up and yelled

Yes! I had heard horror stories about what a difficult person he was to work with and now I saw it with my own eyes. He lived up to every terrible story I had ever heard about him. It was a horrible performance, but I witnessed the train wreck live and in person. Most of the audience wanted their money back from that show.

I heard the next day the governor of South Carolina had come to the show and wanted to meet him backstage. The governor wanted to give Jerry an "Honorary Citizen Award" from the state of South Carolina, but Jerry refused to meet with him. Jerry just got in his car and left.

That was the one and ONLY show he ever played at *The Alabama Theater,* and I saw it! He was never invited back to play there again. I'm not sure if he is even allowed in South Carolina after that.

Years later I went to Memphis. Jerry owns a penthouse apartment on the top of one of the high-rise buildings there overlooking the Mississippi River. At night, if it's dark and the lights are on in the penthouse, you can see a little silhouette of him walking around on the top floor. I saw him one night; he still walked like *Marvin the Martian.*

The Birth Of Jeff Harris

Out of all the fun I had bartending at *Charlie's nightlife* one of the best things that happened to me was I met a guy named Chris Palmer. Chris was a DJ at a local country radio station - Gator 107.9. We eventually talked about the radio experience I had from Pennsylvania. He asked me if I was looking for a job. They needed a midday DJ on his country radio station. I told him, *sure,* I lied again. I had radio experience yes, but as a producer and running the board, not as a jock.

My first day on the air, with my boss standing right behind me, I blurted out the wrong call letters. I said the call letters from the station I used to work at in Pittsburgh. I thought I was fired right then. I guess he knew I was nervous and let it slide and let me find my own style. Once again I bluffed my way through my first shift and soon became the midday disc jockey on the number one country radio station in Myrtle Beach. No one at *Charlie's* new my last name. I was just Jeff to the people who knew me. I needed a last name for on-air. I didn't want to use my real last name on the radio because of situations I had in the past with stalkers. When my boss asked me what name I was going to use, I had two choices. I didn't want the name to be outrageous like Schwarzenegger, so it was going to be either Stone or Harris. Stone was already popular because of the singer Doug Stone at that time. The name Harris came from a girl I knew in college. The two r's in Harris and the two f's in Jeff seemed to fit, so we went with it. And that, my friends is how Jeff Harris was born.

I worked at the radio station for the remaining time I spent in Myrtle Beach. I even went on to receive an award from the South Carolina Association of Broadcasters for being the top midday show in our market. I had the highest midday jock numbers they had ever seen on that radio station. I was proud, and somehow, I pulled it off again. I went from working middays on the country station to doing the afternoon drive on the top 40 radio station that they also owned, just down the hall. My voice was on the airways for eight hours a day from 10a.m. till 6p.m., plus I played music at night at *Charlie's Nightlife*. People were starting to get used to hearing the name "Jeff Harris."

I had a lot of fun working on the radio in Myrtle Beach. I met a lot of people and have a lot of great memories. One afternoon I was working with Chris Palmer. He was doing the afternoon drive on the country station and I was on the rock station. I was chatting with him in his control room when my song ran out on my station. His beeper on his belt went off to notify him that we had "dead air." He turned to me and said, "Is your station off the air?" I peeked out of his control room, looked down the hallway and said *yep* and just continued our conversation. No one ever noticed.

On Monday morning I walked into the office for a staff meeting with the owner. He had established a new policy that we were no longer allowed to wear shorts at work. *Really?* We work on the radio not on TV. We could be bare naked and no one would ever know. The ladies at the station were still allowed to wear their little short business suits, skirts and dresses, but none of the men could wear shorts - and we live at the beach! The next Monday morning I walked into the staff meeting wearing a miniskirt I borrowed from my cousin. The owner looked at me and mouthed something to my boss. My program director asked me what the hell I was doing. I simply replied, *Sir we are allowed to wear skirts to work, just not shorts. What do you think?* He asked me, "Are you serious? I replied *Yes, I am and I'm going to wear one every day from now on.* He then asked if I had shorts in my truck. I replied, *Yeah, I do.* He told me to go put them on and the rule was repealed that very moment. Later on the owner told me the Bulge in the front of my mini skirt was one of the most disturbing things he had ever seen.

I was on the air the day the OJ Simpson verdict was announced. The whole country had been indulged by the trial for months and today was the big day. The control booth was full of staff when my program director told me, "When the verdict comes across the wire, break into whatever song you are playing, rip and read. Got it?" Sure enough in the middle of a song the verdict came in. They handed it to me and it read, "There was an audible gasp in the room as the verdict was read." I killed the song, opened the mic and read *There was audible gas in the room as the verdict was read in the OJ Simpson case.* The whole control room busted out laughing.

After a few years of bartending and working on radio, I was back on stage again, singing and playing and it felt good. I was starting to be known not only from the radio but also for my singing. I played with the band for about a year-and-a-half until I told my girlfriend I wanted to go to Nashville. The time had come for me to move west and give it a shot.

On my last day on radio in Myrtle Beach I signed off my shift and along with a few of the staff, headed across the parking lot to a bar for a goodbye party. The drinks and laughs flowed for hours before calling it a night. In a drunken haze I stumbled back into the radio station. I entered the control room of the top 40 rock station. I wanted to do something and make a statement. In the middle of some random song on the air, maybe *Chumbawamba*? I played Ricky Skaggs *Country Boy* and then followed back to the original format with something like *Hootie and the Blowfish*. It was my final goodbye, so I thought.

In December of 1994 I rented a U-Haul truck. I didn't have enough money saved to pay the cost of a one-way trip to Nashville, so my girlfriend and I loaded the truck with her furniture, loaded my old beat-up 1962 Chevy 10 truck, with a motorcycle on the back, onto a car hauler and we headed west. I unhooked the speedometer on the U-Haul not to show the mileage and drove it to Nashville. My girlfriend and I arrived, unloaded the truck into the new apartment, got a few hours sleep and returned to Myrtle Beach a day and a half later. I reconnected the speedometer, put a few miles on the U-Haul then returned it like it had been a local rental for the weekend. I moved to Nashville for about fifty bucks plus gas. I didn't have a lot of money saved, but my girlfriend got a job in Nashville working for the Red Cross so we at least had some money coming in.

The future was definitely uncertain but exciting, as we began our adventure in Nashville. Even though I will always love Myrtle Beach, it was time to move on. The last thing I did before I left Myrtle Beach was to stop by the radio station on the way out of town. The station was closed, but I still had the codes to get in. They had just gotten new furniture in the lobby a few days earlier. I had sex with my girlfriend on every piece of that new furniture and in the control room before we set out. We pulled out of the parking lot laughing, knowing what we had done. I would give it a few weeks before I revealed what I had done to everyone over the phone. I had christened all the new furniture as a memory of me.

"He Grabbed My Ass"

There is no doubt that my influence and love for Country Music in my life came from my dad.

My father grew up during the birth of Rock n' Roll. While my grandparents listened to big bands and Mom listened to Elvis, my dad had his own taste in music. Dad had a small record collection of his own. He had records like Buddy Knox *Party Doll,* Commander Cody's *Hot Rod Lincoln,* and Buddy Holly from the early Rock n' Roll years. The majority of Dad's records were not Rock n' Roll they were Country Music. Dad loved singers like Hank Williams, Conway Twitty, Loretta Lynn, Tammy Wynette and George Jones. In later years when eight track tapes came out, I remember him buying *Creedence Clearwater Revival,* Charlie Pride and *The Everly Brothers.* Their songs were some of my earliest memories when riding around with Dad in the front seat of his Thunderbird. I distinctly remember singing along with Charlie Pride's *Is Anybody Goin' To San Antone?* Long before seat belts, I would slide back and forth on that front bench seat while we both sang with the windows down. Dad was cool.

Every Saturday night, after watching *Lawrence Welk,* I remember Dad watching *Hee Haw* on TV laughing and singing along with the music and stars of *The Grand Ole Opry* from Nashville. Dad grew up listening to *The Opry* on the radio as a kid and he knew way more about those artists and their songs than I did. He would tell me stories (some made up) and try to give me history lessons and an introduction to Country Music, the songs and the singers. I guess it sunk in.

In 1995 I moved to Nashville from Myrtle Beach and took a job as a stagehand for Gaylord Entertainment. They owned The *Opryland Hotel, Opryland*

Theme Park, The Country Music Hall of Fame, the Ryman Auditorium and The Grand Ole Opry. I spent days working in those locations and had full access to everything as a stagehand. Every Friday and Saturday night while working, I would go backstage at *The Grand Ole Opry* and watch the show from the wings with my radio earpiece in on- standby in case something was needed. Most of the time, I just watched the show. I watched famous *Grand Ole Opry* stars every week and remembered the stories my dad had told me about these performers and their music. They were heroes to him. He had never met any of them or been to *The Opry* until my parents came to visit me in Nashville.

I decided to make my father's lifelong dream come true. Not only was he going to *The Opry* in person with my mom, but I took them through the artist's entrance and brought them backstage. They saw first-hand the behind the scenes interworking of *The Opry*, the dressing rooms, the lockers, the hustle and bustle of *Opry* stars and their bands getting ready to go on stage. Then my parents got to watch them play live. Dad was side by side to some of his musical heroes and could say hello and just get a simple picture. I don't think I have ever seen my dad more happy than that night. I made a lifelong dream come true for him.

Mom was not quite as impressed as my dad was, but that night he got to meet Roy Acuff, Porter Wagoner, Little Jimmy Dickens, Connie Smith and many others while standing on the stage at *The Grand Ole Opry* during the live broadcast. He was in heaven - Country Music Heaven. Backstage at *The Opry* is a hectic place - It is bustling with people everywhere, headed to dressing rooms, the bathroom or make up. They could be tuning up their instruments, warming up their voices, giving interviews, etc. There are artists and their families, TV cameras, production people and a few lucky fans everywhere. There are people constantly coming and going on their way to or from the stage. It's organized chaos!

That night while backstage with my father, I saw *Grand Ole Opry* star and member, Johnny Russell. He had written and had big hit songs like *Act Naturally* (recorded by Buck Owens and *The Beatles*) and *Rednecks, White Socks and Blue Ribbon Beer*. Dad obviously knew who he was when I approached him and asked if he minded taking a picture with my father. He quickly said, "Sure."

What happened next was unexpected, but hilarious. While they were posing for the picture, I was preparing to snap the shot when one of the band members passed behind Johnny and grabbed his ass. I snapped the picture and he quickly moved away from my dad awkwardly. Another person said, "Hey Johnny, what's going on?" He replied, "This guy just grabbed my ass," and pointed at my dad. Johnny then turned and walked away in a hurry. He hadn't seen the band member pass behind and grab him. Johnny thought my father grabbed his ass and was gay.

Dad looked at me in confusion about Johnny's abrupt departure then I explained to him what had just happened. He hadn't seen the band member either. I was the only one who really saw what happened. Dad was horrified, this was his dream of coming to *The Opry* live and seeing his heroes. Now one of them thinks he is gay and just hit on him. Funny stuff, you can't make this shit up.

Every time I hear a Johnny Russell song I think of that night and smile. The rest of the night went off as planned and Dad beamed in the full glory of *The Opry*. He was like a kid at Christmas. On my parents' dresser there is a picture I took that night of my Dad on stage with *The Grand Ole Opry* sign behind him. He looks so happy, and I am glad I could make his wish come true, but it's still not enough to thank him for introducing me to the music I love and perform today.

Ronnie Milsap And Ray Charles

Sometimes you just have to roll with the punches and keep going no matter how bad your timing is. There have been several occasions when I have had some of the most horrible timing. One of those moments is when I kind of met Ronnie Milsap.

One particular morning when I was working in radio in Nashville, I was driving to work and listening to our station. I knew that Ronnie Milsap was coming in that morning to do an interview live on the air. I have always been a big Ronnie Milsap fan and liked his music. I was looking forward to listening to his interview on the radio in my office. I had interviewed Ronnie a few years before in Myrtle Beach and thought him to be a very nice gentleman.

I parked my truck out back of the station and climbed the stairs from the parking garage to my office. My office was on the second floor upstairs from the country station, and just down the hall from the top 40 station. As I entered my office I heard *Hootie and the Blowfish* singing *Everytime I Look At You I Go Blind*. I always loved that song and began to sing along as I realized I had forgotten something in my truck. I left my office and quickly ran down the back staircase to the parking garage singing *Hootie and the Blowfish*. As I burst through the garage door I was singing the words "I Go Blind" at the top of my lungs and bumped face to face into an individual, hard like a hockey check. It was Ronnie Milsap! It was totally an accident, but now I had just ran into him and screamed *I go blind* in his face. His two handlers looked in horror as I quickly said, *sorry,* and rolled off of him like a linebacker on a football field. I kept going, humming the song in complete shock. They continued into the building to do the interview, and after I realized what just happened, I thought to myself, *Wow, my timing sucks. What is the chance of me singing that song and running into Ronnie Milsap, literally.* I don't know if he was mad. Probably not, because it was an accident and he is a nice man, but I didn't worry because I knew he couldn't recognize me.

Before I lived in Key West full-time, I played the winter season for many years. I lived with another seasonal musician, Bil Krauss, at the musician flat on the far side of the island. Bil and I had many good times together as room-mates. We often played practical jokes and enjoyed doing what we called "raccoon reconnaissance." That was watching the family of raccoons at night eating from the nearby resort dumpster. We would shine a flashlight on them, watch their glowing eyes and keep track of how many there were just to pass the time.

One of our favorite things to do was at the end of the winter season. Just before we would head north for the summer, we planned "a night out with Ray," meaning Ray Charles. We would get a group of friends together and head to the local Key West strip clubs and play "Blind Man in a Titty Bar." For the first several years I was the blind man and they named me "Ray." I was the only one who could stay in character the whole time without laughing and giving the gag away.

It was always a great night. At this time the locals did not recognize us on sight and we could walk into the bars like we were typical tourists. With dark glasses on I would enter the strip clubs with my friends and they would lead me right to the rail beside the stage. The dancers would look for a minute and ask the group if I was really blind. They replied, "Yes, he can't see a thing." I would give my money to Bil beforehand and he would hand it back to me. The first year I found out a valuable lesson - give one dollar bills to Bil. The first year he gave me a bill and I held it out in front of me for the dancer. After the dancer took the money, Bil leaned over to me and said, "You're a big tipper Ray, that was a twenty." Damn it! He knew I could not argue about the amount because I was supposed to be blind. He laughed and I told him to knock it off and just give me ones.

I would hold the bill out in my left hand while the strippers were dancing to my right. They would come and rub their boobs all over my face because they thought I couldn't see. It was great. My friends bought me a lap dance and the stripper led me to the back room. I returned a few minutes later with my glasses bent out of shape and so smudged I could barely see out of them. We would stay at the strip club for more drinks before heading out and repeating the same thing at the next one. Good times and laughs all night.

I played "Ray" for several years until my girlfriend said it was time to pass it on to someone else. The last year we did the "Blind Man in a Titty Bar," we passed the duties onto Bil's Uncle Wade. Wade wore an eye patch anyway because he needed it. He was an actor as well and he could play the part. He did great.

The Road To Europe

When I made the move to travel to Europe to play for the first time I was at a bad place in my life. The year before I had lost my father to a sudden heart attack, broke up with my girlfriend of three years and lost my job in radio. I didn't really mind leaving radio. It was all about the advertising money and no longer about the music. I had gotten into radio for the music and my experience of it had been stained by the almighty dollar. Although I didn't like it at the end, it was my income. Now I had none. No job, rent to pay and a dog to feed who ate more than I did. During those times, Ubu my dog and I ate a lot of White Castle burgers with free coupons I had left over from a radio promotion. I needed a job. Musical gigs were hard to find in Nashville, especially paying gigs, and there was no way to survive on music.

I took a job working at a titty bar as a DJ for fifty dollars a night to try and survive. I worked only four nights a week and things were getting bad. I was having trouble making rent and the utilities were slowly being turned off one by one. I needed a decent job or I was going to have to move back to Pennsylvania with my mom, with my tail between my legs. It looked as though I was going to go back home and do construction again.

Late one night, in desperation, I was searching for musical booking agents online, looking for anyone who could get me a gig, and a little money for food and gas and hopefully a place to sleep. A site came up that said "Booking Agent UK." I thought to myself, *I've never been to the UK before or Europe. I have always wanted to see Europe and if I can make enough money to cover my expenses and have a lifetime experience why the hell not.?* At this point I had nothing to lose. I had just turned thirty. I was dating a lovely girl at the time who had three beautiful daughters, but she was looking for someone to be a father to her girls and I was not ready for that. I could not be a good male role model to them. I could barely take care of myself and Ubu.

I sent a one-line email to the agent that read, *Can you keep a solo act busy?* That was it. A few days later I got a reply that said, "Yeah if you're good." I smiled and immediately knew that this agent somehow got me. Her name was Emma. She was from England and her husband was a Norwegian musician named Christian. She knew musicians and understood what we needed and went through, so now she was booking too. I sent her a press kit, bio, picture and my latest CD in the mail. In a few weeks she got back to me and offered me six weeks on a circuit of bars in Copenhagen, Denmark. I spoke briefly with her and her husband over the phone about my questions and concerns, but they assured me I would be okay. The other musicians would help me along the way and I would be fine. I was scheduled to play six nights a week, four sets a night. I would be provided a place to stay with the other musicians. I was entitled to one meal a day from the bar and at the end of the month I would be paid in cash provided they liked me, and I didn't get fired. I would be paid about one hundred and twenty dollars a night. It was more than my DJ job at the strip club and way more than any gig paying in Nashville. All I had to do was pay for my flight over and back. There was no guarantee on the gig; if I sucked and got fired I was headed back home and would go even more broke from the plane fare. That was another problem. I didn't have enough money to buy the ticket to get there. In my dire financial struggle, I had to sell my motorcycle, which I loved dearly, bought a ticket to Copenhagen and accepted the gig.

So in May of 2000 I'd dropped my best friend, Ubu, off with my mom and boarded the plane for Denmark.

In hindsight it was career suicide. I was flying across the globe to play six weeks, maybe, in a country that I knew very little about. I had only ever been out of the U.S. to Niagara Falls, Canada, and there they spoke English. I had to look Denmark up on a globe.

I didn't know Danish. How was I going to read it or speak it? What kind of music would they want to hear? What would the sound system or bars be like? What about the food, the transportation, the sleeping quarters? I knew nothing. I was flying blind with nothing but a guitar case, a backpack and a suitcase full of clothes. I was told there was another American musician named

Kenneth who lived in Copenhagen who would meet me at the airport. He would take me to the musician flat. With the hope that everything went well, I would be paid at the end of the month. I was scared to death. I believe I even cried a little bit on the plane.

I flew from Pittsburgh, to Detroit then to London Heathrow and finally Copenhagen. I was completely lost and in culture shock. The hassle of getting through customs and security in other countries was new to me. I finally arrived in Copenhagen about noon Danish time. For the first time I was walking through a European airport seeing signs everywhere that I could not understand. Well of course not, they were in Danish. I quickly learned some words were in English, but it was easier just to follow the arrows and the other people who were on my plane. As soon as we exited the door of the plane and we're walking down the tunnel, a guy lit up a cigarette and started smoking. Things were a little different here.

I found my way to the baggage claim and headed for the exit. After leaving the secure area, I spotted Kenneth holding a little piece of paper that just said "Jeff." He walked up to me and introduced himself. "First time huh? Welcome." Then he laughed. I asked how he knew it was me. He replied, "You have a guitar case and look lost," as we headed for the taxi. He briefly gave me a rundown and tried to comfort my obvious nervousness as we were looking around as we drove to the flat. When the cab stopped, I took some of the little money I had and tried to pay the cab driver with a U.S. twenty dollar bill. The driver looked at me like I was crazy. Kenneth laughed and said, "I got this one." In my defense I was told they would accept American currency, but that was not the case at all. I needed to get some of my money exchanged into Danish Kroner. Now I'd have to learn new money and its value. I felt like a fool as the cab pulled away. I was definitely out of my comfort zone as Kenneth punched in the passcode and we entered the flat.

Whenever I see him, Kenneth still gives me shit about trying to pay a Danish cab driver with an American twenty dollar bill.

The Flat

What can I say about it other than I have spent some of the best times of my life in that dump? The actual name was "the musician flat" but we all just called it "the flat." It was more like *Animal House,* or as I like to refer to it "guitar player summer camp." There were eight men and occasionally women from different countries all living under the same roof for a month at a time while playing various bars across Copenhagen. Most of the time the personalities mixed well and occasionally they didn't, but I have met some of the best friends I will ever have there.

The flat was an illegal apartment on the third floor of a warehouse building in an industrial neighborhood of Copenhagen. The outside of the building was gray brick, stained and unkempt to say the least. The inside was no better. The flat was on the third floor with no elevator which always made for a good time arriving with heavy suitcases and guitar gear. The stairway always smelled like a men's gym locker room. It just added to the anticipation of what might be going on upstairs. Once you opened that door to the main room it was like *Alice in Wonderland.* You never knew who or what you were going to find. And I have seen a lot.

The main common area had a rectangular dining table and about eight chairs, two sofas, a coffee table, and there was a TV that did not have cable, roughly just hooked to a VCR player where we all watched movies. It had two gigantic speakers that look like they came from a 1970's stereo system that someone had bought from the flea market. Sometimes they worked?

Along the main wall was a bookshelf full of books, movies, guitar strings, rolling papers, pipes and other odds and ends left behind by former traveling musicians. The wall was covered with one of the finest works of art I have ever seen. It had pictures of different musicians from everywhere who had played there over the years. All the pictures were taken in random time complete with a hysterical caption underneath to add to the beauty of the moment. Musicians are very creative people by nature, especially when we are bored on the road. We can come up with some very funny, clever stuff. There were also local news clippings from time to time about funny things we didn't understand. There were some things that just made us laugh. It was a truly eclectic piece and it set the tone for any new musician of what was about to come in the near future. Once you made "The Wall of Shame" you were in the family. I could stare at that wall for hours, year after year and still laugh and find things I've never seen before. It was truly a great collage and one of a kind. It belonged in a *Hard Rock Cafe* somewhere. So did that table. Sadly the collection was torn down one night by a musician that felt it might be offensive and inappropriate for his girlfriend. What a Dick!

Across the room, the wall next to the TV had a big poster of Jimi Hendrix on it. It made the place look musically decorated but actually the poster was covering a hole in the wall. Some musicians had a beer bottle breaking contest one night and put a hole in the wall so we had to cover it up. Seems strange now in hindsight, but that kind of stuff could happen any day.

The table that was in the flat also should have been in a *Hard Rock Cafe* somewhere. The parties that have happened around that table were legend-ary in true "Rockstar" form. It was not unusual to wake up in the morning and look at that table like it was a crime scene out of an episode of CSI. When you looked at the objects that were left there from the night before, you could tell what kind of night it was. On a typical morning you could find an ashtray overflowing with several different kinds of cigarette butts, half smoked joints, empty bottles of liquor, wine or beer, empty cigarette packs, dead lighters, matches, cards, small bits of hash, an empty bag of pot, reading glasses and half-eaten food and more. I have actually taken pictures of that table in the morning after. It truly was a work of art.

On the other side of the room was the "kitchen," and I use that term loosely. It had a stove with two hot plates that sometimes worked, a sink usually full of dirty dishes, a microwave, a toaster oven and a tea kettle for hot water. We used an ironing board for a bread-cutting table and the fridge was disgusting. It smelled of old food left there by musicians past. We had no idea whose it was or how long it had been in there. Limburger cheese stinks already, but it's especially bad if it's been in there a while. We have been known to put toilet paper in the fridge for the next morning after someone had made a batch of Texas Chili the night before. It's actually a good idea, it eases the burning. You just never knew what was going to be in that fridge, but you knew it hadn't been cleaned for a long time.

Somehow we made do with the only things we had on hand. Occasionally one of us would buy some new pots or dishes from the flea market or somewhere and try to add to the supply, but most of the dishes were old and worn out. I usually bought paper plates, it was just easier.

I remember a lot of things about the flat. There were always burned out lights. We had to get new light bulbs from the bars where we played and we always forgot. There were rarely clean bed linens or towels; you usually had to walk to the laundromat to wash them yourself when you arrived. There was a windowsill full of beer and wine bottles waiting to be returned to the market for recycling so you could buy more beer. There was a market a few blocks away, the bus stop, a bakery, a convenience store that sold porn movies, a pizza shop, barber shop and a laundromat. We had all we needed to survive and we did for years.

I can only imagine what the neighbors thought of us. They never saw us in the daylight. We usually stayed up all night, sometimes till six in the morning, then slept all day and only emerged after dark. One by one, or maybe two, we appeared all dressed in black, carrying something that "looked like" a guitar. We would disappear into the night only to return late again. They must have thought we were some kind of terrorist group or hit squad.

One of my favorite memories of the flat is the time we threw a surprise birthday party for one of my friends, Duncan Gillies. Duncan was a legend at that flat. A lifelong musician from Scotland, he had worked the Copenhagen circuit for years. He lived at the flat most of the time and was the only constant thing that ever went on there. He had worked every one of the gigs and could give us guidance about the gig or where we needed to go. He was like the "house mother." At times he was almost impossible to understand with his thick Scottish accent until you got used to it. We all loved him dearly and still do.

One time he had mentioned to me that his birthday was coming up in a few weeks and he'd never had a birthday party in his whole life. I got with the other musicians and we decided to throw him a surprise party. For a few weeks we put the word out to other musicians, bar staff and friends about our plan to throw him a bash and keep it hush hush. We stocked up booze in our rooms for a week or so. My buddy, Mick, actually distilled Sangria in his room for about a week. When you entered his room you could get a buzz just by breathing. We gathered everything we needed and the plan was in place. As soon as we finished our gigs we would hurry home to surprise Duncan for his birthday. He had the night off and would be out having a few, so we planned to get home before him. He talked for days about "You know my birthday is coming up," and we all just blew him off like it was no big deal. Duncan was going to be surprised.

That night we all hurried home after our gigs for the big party. There must have been thirty people. Musicians, bartenders, waitresses and friends, we all waited for Duncan. And we waited, and we waited. Finally, it occurred to us that no one had been in charge of bringing Duncan to the party.

We were throwing a party for him and no one knew where he was? We finally tracked him down when we phoned *The Olde English Pub*. He was sitting there all alone drinking with the bartender, closing the place down in sadness because nobody remembered it was his birthday. The bartender told him, "Hey let's grab a cab, go to the flat and have a beer to celebrate your birthday." So hours after the party started "the Man of Honor" finally walked through the door to find a room of friends who loved him. He was totally surprised and happy. We made his birthday! We all had gifts, mostly ridiculous stuff, bought from the flea market or stolen from the bars where we played. Simple gifts, including a pink toilet seat mirror that was signed by *The Beatles*. Okay it wasn't really *The Beatles*. The signatures we did ourselves, but it was the thought that counts. The party went on for hours and we had fun and laughs galore. It was such a good night. As the party faded out around nine in the morning, Duncan was the last man standing in a hula skirt we had made him from a trash bag. It was his birthday and he was partying like a "Rockstar." The hangovers from that night lasted for days.

There are so many stories about this flat. Everyone who was ever there has at least one or more. Another one that sticks out in my mind is the night two musicians got stopped by the police on the way home from their gig. The police wanted to see their passports. The two didn't have their passports on them, they were at the flat. The police followed them home to see in person. The musicians were panicking as they already knew that we lived in an illegal flat, and some of the musicians living there did not have all their appropriate paperwork for being in the country. Not to mention the two musicians also knew the flat and what went on there almost every night; the parties, the drinking, the drugs and more. Now the cops were coming unannounced and about to find God knows who and what? We were all going to be in trouble. This was before everyone had cell phones to contact each other. There was no warning, the cops would just walk in the room and bust all the musicians and whatever we were doing. The two musicians prepared for the worst. When they got there I was lying on the sofa in the common room all alone watching a movie. Everyone else was in bed or not at home yet. The house was quiet except for the sound of the TV. I was surprised by the presence of cops, but the two guys just showed their passports, answered a few questions and the cops left. The two musicians put their guitars down, sat at the table and breathed a big sigh of relief. They explained what happened and why we had cops there. The good news was we escaped without a problem. All was quiet. The fact of the matter was we just had a big party the night before in true "Rockstar" style and everyone was tired and hungover and had gone to bed early. Dumb luck. I had smoked a joint and turned on a movie about an hour before the cops had arrived. Thankfully there was no party that night, we got lucky. After that a few other musicians showed up and we filled them in on what just happened. We all had a good laugh, a deep sigh of relief and celebrated our narrow Escape with a joint and drinks.

There was a time we had a dog living at the flat. We were already there illegally and if the owner knew we had a dog he would shit. This dog, a big-ass Greyhound, belonged to one of the other players and his girlfriend. The dog was sweet and shy, but she was big. It took up almost the entire sofa for a bed. When they fed that dog they made pounds of ground meat, pasta and all sorts of other "dog stuff." They cooked it up in a big pot and let it cool for the dog's meal. That Greyhound ate better than most of us musicians by far. One afternoon one of the other weird guys on the circuit (I can't remember his name) came out of his room and saw the pot on the stove. No one else was around, and at times beer and food were plundered and pillaged in that flat. He got a spoon and began to inhale the goodness in that pot. One of the others came out of the shower and saw him. He said, "Sorry man, I'm just so hungry, I have no food or money and I just wanted something to eat. I only took a little." The other musician just passing through on the way back to his room said, "You know that's dog food right?" He was just a weird guy!

There were a lot of great times and conversations had around that table, but the thing I remember most is the fellowship and respect of my brother and sister musicians. We were like a dysfunctional family. We all helped each other, showed each other different songs or guitar licks, talked about music and influences, talked about family, told jokes and stories of the road and life in general. There were never any egos involved. The friends I have made there in that flat turned out to be some of my closest friends I will ever have in my life, and I am forever grateful.

The last time I stayed at the old flat was July of 2013. I had not played Copenhagen for about six years. A lot of the musicians had come and gone and in that time the old place had definitely gone downhill, even worse than it was before, if that was possible. There were suitcases and boxes full of things lining the hallways outside of the rooms. Things of all kinds had been left behind by previous players to retrieve if they ever returned. It was filthy and it looked and smelled bad. At this point I had been fortunate enough in my career that I could afford to purchase some things needed for that flat that I could never afford before. I went to the market, bought some cleaning supplies, bleach, a brush and rubber gloves. I returned to clean a bit while the guys were still asleep. Just trying to be a good guy and pay the good karma forward, I swept and mopped the floor, cleaned the table from the night before, scrubbed the toilets and even the showers, which is why I bought the rubber gloves. The boys woke up and came out of their rooms to a clean flat that smelled like bleach. They would comment, "What's that smell?" I replied, *bleach,* to which they said, "Wow, never smelled that in here before!"

As I write this chapter, I am in my room in the "new musicians flat." That's right - after more than twenty years we finally got an upgrade. We still live in a warehouse building, but we all have our own rooms complete with hardwood floors, new beds, new pillows and linens, a desk and chair, lights that actually work and lockers from the old flat. The showers downstairs are clean and don't smell. We even have Wi-Fi, a long way from the days when we had to take a bus to the internet cafe and pay money just to check or send email. The new flat is like a "bull pen," a far cry from the old "pig pen" we used to live in. I like to think of our new flat as "the office." We all have our own little office where we sleep, watch TV or movies, and work on our computers. If you're awake, you leave your door cracked open and anyone is allowed to knock and come into your office. We have no common area anymore where we used to have all the parties. (There's probably a good reason behind that.) Maybe it's a good thing as we have all gotten older. Nowadays when we return from working late night we all just fade off to our offices and go to sleep. Although I still miss the time sitting around that table for a bit, unwinding after the show, it's okay. I feel like we are finally being treated more like the professionals we are and it's a good feeling. To quote Tracy Lawrence, "*Time Marches On.*"

Currently the hot water went out and we are waiting for it to be fixed. Since it's the weekend, God only knows when that will happen? None of us have showered in days. Some things never change.

I think I'll take a trip past the old flat today. They are remodeling it. Guess they are going to make it comfortable and nice? A far cry from what it was when we lived there.

The Flat 2000.

First Gig In Europe

I wish I could say my first twenty-four hours in Copenhagen were good. Some memories yes, but the majority of the first twenty-four hours was rough. After I wrestled my bags up three flights of stairs to the musician flat, I was politely introduced to some of the musicians who lived there and we're awake. I had just met Kenneth for the first time at the airport, then met Rocky from Washington, D.C., a Scottish guy named Duncan (who I couldn't understand a word he was saying with his thick accent) and an Australian bloke named Andy.

The best way to describe Andy is like Bob Dylan and a cartoon character had a child. He was a troubadour on the circuit, a songwriter and an actor as well. He was very animated and funny whatever he did. He had a wicked sense of humor and a thick Aussie accent.

Andy was playing at the bar where I would be playing. He was to show me how to get there on the bus, fill me in on the gig, show me where the equipment was located and get me "sorted out" so they say. He introduced me to the bar manager, Dennis, who I had been warned about by the other musicians. He was strict, and the right-hand man of the rich man who owned all the bars I would be playing in. Keep on your toes and do a good job.

After Andy set up for the gig, he came to the bar and asked me if I wanted a beer. At this point I had been up for about thirty hours straight and my nerves were shot. I was in culture shock, I was lost, I just moved into a room at the flat that looked like a prison cell. I was clueless about what the gig was going to be like. Coffee or beer? At this point, I didn't care. I was exhausted!

Our conversation went like this…

Andy - "You want a beer, mate?"

Me - *Okay, give me a beer.*

Andy - "What kind?"

Me - *I don't care, give me a Budweiser. (*It was the only thing I recognized.)

Andy - "You can't drink that *shite*, mate, you're in Europe. Have a good beer. Do you want an Elephant Beer?"

Me - *Huh?*

Andy - "Have you ever had an Elephant Beer?"

Me - *No.*

Andy - "They're the best, mate. You gotta try one."

Me - *Okay, give me an Elephant Beer.*

What I didn't know was "Elephant Beer" is 7.5% alcohol. It was loaded and heavier than a Colt 45 Malt Liquor which is between 5 and 6%. Andy was baptizing me to the circuit without me knowing. He proceeded to feed me those beers all night long and I just kept drinking them. I thought that was what everyone else was drinking. I later found out – no, they were drinking normal beer. Andy was intentionally getting me hammered.

I watched Andy perform songs by Bob Dylan, Simon and Garfunkel and a lot of *Creedence Clearwater Revival*. I felt like I might be able to fake my way through this. I didn't recognize all the songs he played, but I could probably squeeze my way through the show tomorrow night and then pick up some new songs. I kept watching Andy and he kept feeding me Elephant Beers.

After his gig ended, he took me to another bar two doors down called *The Old English Pub*. He introduced me to my new agent, Emma. Right from the moment I saw her she was stunning, with short blonde hair and a smile that lit up the room. She spoke with a lovely English accent and she asked me if I would like to have a beer. Andy replied, "He's drinking Elephant Beer tonight." She and Andy both chuckled. She was very sweet and welcomed me to the circuit. I was to meet up with her tomorrow in the daytime. She wanted to show me around, help me get money exchanged, buy a phone card and take me to a place called Christiania, a place I had never heard of before. She said she would see me tomorrow as Andy and I finished our beers and headed out the door to another bar.

Every town has that one little bar that is dark, drunken and smoky. The only time you go there is when it's late and you know you're already hammered. Andy had been feeding me Elephant Beers all night and I was drunk and exhausted by the time he took me to my first visit at *The Hong Kong Bar.*

It was at the other end of the walking street from the *Old English Pub* on the canal in an area called New Haven. (Pronounced new hound.) After a fifteen-minute walk down a cobblestone walking street right through the center of Copenhagen, we finally made it. I had never seen it before and that fifteen-minute walk seemed like a long way in the drunk and darkness, but there we were at last. We entered New Haven, a long strip of bars and restaurants with outdoor seating right on the canal, a lovely place in the daytime, but at night it comes alive with drinking and parties all night long. Andy took me to the doorway to the downstairs of *The Hong Kong.* Upstairs was a titty bar and downstairs there was a smoky-fog of a bar room with a jukebox playing, and drunk people crammed into this tiny basement. I don't know how long we stayed. Andy was used to being up all night and sleeping during the day. To the best of my recollection we walked out of there about 6 a.m.

The sun was up and Andy remarked, "Holy shit, that sun is bright." Of course it was! We were out ALL night and spent several hours in a drunken basement. In Denmark at that time the sun is out for all but maybe six hours of darkness.

We somehow made it to a bus and arrived back at the flat about eight in the morning. We said good night and Andy went off to bed.

I returned to "my cell" and was ready to just crash hard and get some much-needed sleep. It was still cold outside, but the owner had turned off the heat because he said it was summer and he wouldn't pay for it again till fall. Sure, it was summer to them, but it was freezing to me as I lay down fully dressed from the cold trying to stay warm and not die of hypothermia. Not long after I lay down, "The Elephant" came into the room, then I knew I was going to be sick. I jumped up and darted out of my room for the shared bathroom at the other end of the hall. I barely made it as I puked my guts out and all the Elephant Beer. That toilet was nasty and now I had my face in it, but I didn't care. I spent the rest of that morning throwing up about every fifteen minutes, the same thing over and over. I would puke, flush, and piss because I had been drinking beer all night; puke, flush and piss again, repeat. At this point my head was pounding and I was puking like a fountain when I felt The Rumble in my stomach.

One thing I have learned about traveling abroad is you must be careful of the water. Although you can drink as much bottled water as you want, some of the local water will still get into your system. Coffee, tea, food, ice or whatever, you are eventually going to ingest some of that foreign water. Therefore, you're going to get the shits. It still happens to me the first two weeks out of my own country or for two weeks after returning home I get diarrhea. It sucks, but there is really nothing you can do about it. It's bound to happen, so prepare to spend a lot of time on *the throne* and deal with it. I have been known to eat Imodiums like M&Ms.

At that point I was dizzy, my head was pounding, I was puking what was left of my guts out and now I had the shits. Where the fuck am I?

I don't know how many times I went back and forth down that hallway from my room to the bathroom that day. It was a lot and I barely got any sleep. That afternoon Andy took me to the town center to get a bus pass and meet up with Emma. He knew I was feeling like shit and I looked bad. I hadn't had a shower in two days and I had just been up puking and shitting. The Hangover was setting in and The Elephant got me.

We stopped at a 7-Eleven and Andy bought a pack of smokes. I was so sick I decided I NEEDED something to eat. I hadn't had anything since I arrived in Denmark. I bought a Gatorade and a banana which I thought might help. We walked across the main square in Copenhagen while I ate my banana and drank my Gatorade. Halfway through the square I took off running for a garbage can. I thrust my face forward and puked again. I threw up the banana and Gatorade until there was nothing left in my system to come out. What a sorry sight I was with my head in that trash can in the middle of the main square, but at this point I didn't care anymore. "Stupid American Tourist." Yeah, that was me and Andy just watched and laughed his ass off.

When I finished he said, "How you feeling, Elephant Man, you need another beer?" On our way to meet Emma he filled me in on the fact that Elephant Beer has a high amount of alcohol and he knew it. He wouldn't drink that shit, but he fed it to me because he was *taking the piss out of me.*

He passed me on to Emma and fucked off on his merry way to leave me deal with my hangover. I met Emma and her husband, Christian, and they took me to see Christiania.

We spent an hour or so together, they showed me around the important places I needed to know, and filled me in on the gig. Emma told me she would come see my show later that night. We parted and I returned home to the flat to try and get some sleep and get ready for my European debut. I got a brief nap then woke up still feeling like complete shit. I showered, changed my clothes, grabbed my guitar and headed for the bus to my first gig.

I was sick in my stomach, couldn't eat, I had the shakes, cold sweats and the shits. Now I have to play in front of my new agent for the first time. I was about to face an audience that I had NO idea how to speak their language or know what they wanted to hear. To say the least I was a nervous wreck inside when I started playing Simon and Garfunkel's *Homeward Bound*. I toughed it through the evening, watching the audience to see what they reacted to. Some songs they knew and liked, some songs they didn't, but I was able to fake my way through. I also learned that Danish people don't always clap at the end of the song. Sometimes there is just an awkward silence and bar chatter when the music stops.

After my first show, I sat with Emma and waited to see what she thought. Was I okay? Could I do the job? Or was I headed home? She informed me that I did okay and I would be fine. I had the gig! She knew I felt like shit from the night before, she could see that I was exhausted, jet lagged, pale and nervous, but she knew what Andy had done to me the night before. She never said a word about it. She knew that he was welcoming *the rookie* to the circuit and it all would work out okay.

I spent the next six weeks exploring Copenhagen. The other musicians showed me around, they showed me songs and guitar licks. I learned new songs that fit the shows and tried to understand the Danish and their culture. All went well. I said previously that from a logistical standpoint, it was career suicide for me to go on this tour. Looking back now, I can say it was one of the best things that has ever happened to me in my life. Yeah, I was scared, but I was introduced to a whole new world. I was inducted into a musical brotherhood like I had never seen. I made friends that I will have for the rest of my life and wonderful memories that go with them. We have shared conversations and stories about music, friends, family and life. A brotherhood of fellow musicians from all over the world. We share that bond and I will be forever grateful for every one of them, for the most part.

If it hadn't been for those six weeks in Copenhagen, I would have never known a different way of life. As I left Copenhagen I realized I was going to miss it and began to plan for another trip abroad as soon as I could. If it hadn't been for that first trip to Denmark, I would have never met my wife on tour years later in Europe, nor would I have our son and the family and friends I do now.

I will always have a special place in my heart for Denmark and Copenhagen for many reasons. I played my first gig outside of my own country there, I started a new chapter of my life there and on New Year's Eve 2002, my wife and I had our first date there. I considered Copenhagen to be *The Jewel of Scandinavia*. Maybe that is why I have played there so many times and often return. Copenhagen is almost spiritual for me. Although my first twenty four hours there sucked, I still love that town.

Oh, and just for the record, Andy still calls me "The Elephant Man."

Christiania

It's like a little magical oasis in the middle of Copenhagen. I feel like a kid walking through the walls of Disneyland when I go there. Christiania is a place like nowhere else in the world I have ever been.

It's located on the site of an old Danish military fortress built in the tenth century. A self-contained little city complete with housing, shops and more, it's all inside a big surrounding wall. In later years the Danish military had moved onto new accommodations and left the place to collapse on its own. In the late Sixties, during the decade of "free love," hippies moved into the unused city and set up home and society.

For years it has been a political issue over their rights to be there. Technically, Denmark owns the land and they are trespassing. The Christianians are resilient and claim they have squatter's rights and have set up their own society inside those walls. They actually claimed to be a separate territory from Denmark and claimed to be free. There are actually signs as you leave the exits of Christiania reading, "You are now entering the EU." I love it!

Over the years of inhabiting their little space, they have set up a government for the commune. General rules and regulations apply to ALL who live there and those who enter. They have a security staff, restaurants, cafes and coffee shops. There are businesses that sell artsy, hippie stuff, a shop that builds bicycles (some of the coolest bikes in the world,) schools, daycares, soccer fields, they grow their own food, recycle and much more. There is a band shell for live entertainment and a few bars. They have a population of an estimated eight hundred residents who live in old homes, some built or repaired out of recycled goods. There are dogs roaming free everywhere that are actually famous called *Christiania Dogs*. It is peaceful, and a true "Hippies' Paradise".

JEFF HARRIS

Near the band shell is an outside picnic table area with a cafe called
Nemoland. I have spent many an hour there, people watching, reading a
book, drinking coffee and just enjoying a Danish summer day. At any given
day or night you can find people of any color, young and old; it doesn't matter.
You might see anything from suits to school kids, burnouts to moms with
kids in strollers, businessmen doing big deals while tourist groups walk past.
Everyone is cool, polite, laid-back and kind.

One of the reasons that everyone is so chill is because the biggest thing that
Christiania is known for is *Pusher Street*. It's about a one hundred yard long
section of the main street that runs down through the center of the fortress.
Along each side of the narrow street are roughly built plywood booths, side
by side, selling *Soft Drugs,* marijuana, hash and hallucinogenic mushrooms.
Each booth is lined with Tupperware containers labeled with its distinct flavor.
Orange Haze, White Widow, Jimi Hendrix, White Russian, Danish Skunk and
more. (I would love to have the job of the guy that names the pot.) There are
bricks of hash that lay on the table for display, also with equally funny names.
They looked like a lump of fudge.

The first time I ever saw hash I was blown away. My agent, Emma, took
me there whenever I first arrived in Denmark. She showed me the ropes of
the place. I was too embarrassed to ask, but after a few minutes I realized
that the fudge-looking thing on the table was actually hash. I had never seen
it before. Bowls of mushrooms were on display on the tables at a few of the
shops. They had pre-rolled joints and nice little tubes, all the goodies right at
your fingertips, but that was it.

I mentioned the term *Soft Drugs* but there are two kinds. There are also
Hard Drugs. The difference is *Soft Drugs* are anything that comes from the
earth naturally, not chemically related or processed. *Hard Drugs* such as
cocaine, ecstasy, heroin, crack and anything else like it are not allowed in
Christiania. Anyone caught trying to sell that bad stuff will immediately be
beaten up, thrown out and banned from Christiania by their society forever.
It's not pretty and they are strict, they don't fuck around. The same thing would
happen if you were caught trying to sneak a picture or a video. For obvious
reasons you are not allowed to film or take pictures while you are there. The
dealers do not want to be seen on camera. I have seen and heard stories of

how they have taken people's cameras or phones and erased ALL the pictures or just smashed it into the ground.

On my first trip there with my agent, we bought a joint and headed to the picnic tables at the cafe by the band shell. As a *Blues Brothers* tribute band played in the background we smoked that joint. Twenty minutes later I was high as a kite. That joint hit me like a bus. That was good, strong stuff, a lot better than the loose, dirt-farm grown stuff I was used to smoking in America. This was real shit. That day I was hooked, not on drugs but on Christiania. I loved the lifestyle of the people, the music, the love and peace. It was a day I will never forget.

And now I need to point out something. Yes, marijuana is a drug and I have smoked it for years but I don't do other drugs, never have, and I have no desire. However, I do smoke cigarettes.

For years I have been told the dangers of marijuana being a gateway drug, leading to heavier or more dangerous drugs. It did! It led me to cigarettes. Yes, I say cigarettes and nothing more. For years I have gotten repeated, judging comments and shit about being a smoker and a singer. Yeah, yeah, yeah, in my defense, being a musician, there are a lot of other worse things I can put in my body other than a cigarette, but I don't. I did not smoke until I was thirty-two years old. Prior to that, I hated cigarettes. I didn't like the smell or the taste. I found them disgusting. My father smoked when I was a kid, I hated it, and I swore I would never smoke cigarettes. This is how it happened.

In America when we smoke marijuana we smoke it pure and straight. Whether in a pipe, joint or bong, we smoke just the "marijuana bud" and nothing else. In Europe they roll their own joints with a mix of pot or hash and cigarette tobacco. It takes less of a drug to get the buzz and the tobacco makes the joint burn better. I began smoking joints with tobacco in them and got nicotine in my system. It's that simple, I blame Europe for my smoking. Yes, marijuana led me to cigarettes.

Now back to Christiania. As I mentioned, I have spent many an afternoon there; people watching, reading books, writing or learning new songs, watching bands, lovers, dogs and hippies. The fresh air and sun is always magical.

The nighttime gets a little more seedy, but still okay. If we musicians went there after dark, we always went by two or more together. We all knew where it was and had been there many times. Each one of us had our favorite dealer who would hook us up with a little extra for being a returning customer. We all had our own preferences of what we liked, whether it be pot or hash, it was your flavor of choice, just like a *Baskin-Robbins* of pot.

One of my favorite hazy memories of Christiania is the night my future best man, Mick and I went to *The Woodstock Cafe.* After our gigs that night, we decided to head to "The Big C" as Mick called it, and get one of our favorite joints, *The Laughing Cobra.* It cost a hundred Danish Kroner (about twelve bucks,) and it was pre-rolled and ready to go. This was a funny fucking snake. Mick is from Cork City, Ireland, and has a funny sense of humor anyway. When we smoked this joint, things just got hysterical for hours; the two of us would laugh and laugh and laugh.

After we bought the joint, we headed to the cafe about 3 a.m. It was wintertime and cold as a witch's tit in Scandinavia, so we took a cab from our gigs to Christiania then walked the rest of the way to the café on *pusher street.* We went inside, grabbed two beers, then sat down at the end of a picnic table and smoked away.

The room was packed full of people. All the wooden picnic tables that filled the room were full. People were standing around the room and at the bar. It was filled with smoke, loud conversation and background music. After "The Snake" began to kick in, Mick looked around and realized we were the only "white people" in the room. The whole bar was full of what we believed to be people from the Faroe Islands, which are located off the coast of Scotland. The people of the Faroe Islands have different features than typical Caucasians. They have more of a Native Indian/Eskimo look, and Mick and I were definitely not in the majority. Nobody bothered us, but we were alone in there and probably pretty paranoid by this time.

We finished our beers and decided to head home. We left the table and walked out the front door, and even though it was quite a chilly night, there were still a bunch of people milling around the front porch. Suddenly Mick noticed a set of crutches leaning against the wall unattended. Mick looked at me and said, "Watch this." He walked over, took one of the crutches and began to limp away. I was laughing my ass off trying not to be seen. He had just stolen someone's crutch, some poor son of a bitch with a broken leg is going to limp out of that bar and find he has only one crutch. He was going to be pissed and we needed to go. It was hysterical at the time but a bit dodgy. Mick limped on his crutch while we strolled back through *pusher street*, laughing towards the exit. When we got to the entrance where the cab had dropped us off, Mick left the crutch and there we stood, freezing in the middle of the night.

Busses didn't run to Christiania much late at night. There was no metro back then and it was too far to walk to our flat. Our only hope was that a taxi would randomly pass by and pick us up. We stood there for what must have been forty five minutes or longer, freezing, shivering, jumping up and down to keep warm while wobbling and still laughing from "The Snake" - completely stoned. After what seemed like forever waiting for a cab that never came, Mick said, "Hey Jeffrey, guess what I have? A phone!" then pulled it out of his jacket. I replied, *Guess what? so do I!* We decided that maybe it was a better idea to call a cab from our phones then wait for one to pass by. Brilliant idea! After an hour of standing in the cold we realized we had phones; "The Snake" got us! In ten minutes time we were in a nice warm cab on our way to the neighborhood bakery and then home to bed. In hindsight, it was a hysterically stoned episode that we still laugh about today, but of course it was. It was *The Laughing Cobra*!

Christiania is a magical, wonderful place and the best part is not many people know about it. It's not known worldwide like Amsterdam. It's small, sweet, unforgettable and mostly unknown.

If you are ever in Copenhagen, I recommend you go visit. You can take guided tours or just go on your own. It's open 24/7. You don't have to do drugs or smoke. No one would judge you if you did or didn't. Just enjoy the life experience, culture and traditions.

One of my favorite views in the world is from the top of the steps behind *Nemoland* overlooking the lake. When I feel sad, I picture that view in my head and it makes me happy. I hope someday you might have a wonderful memory of Christiania in your life like I do.

If you ever do go to Christiania, stop by *Nemoland*, and look for *King Arthur's Sword* sticking out of the rock and enjoy. But beware of *The Laughing Cobra*, it is one funny fucking snake.

Lost In Translation

Throughout my life, my career has given me the opportunity to travel to many different countries. Being born American, I always tell people I speak three languages: American English, Redneck and Drunken Redneck, which were all different. In my line of work the only thing I need to learn to say in a foreign language is hello, excuse me, thank you, drink and good night. After that, I move on to a different country and the language I've just spoken is lost.

My first gig out of my own country was in Copenhagen, Denmark. While in Denmark I met a lot of wonderful musicians. On one of my first tours there I met a young Swedish musician named Mats. He was in his early twenties, quiet, very talented and had a dry sense of humor. With all of us other players in the room, Mats was the "young pup" and usually sat quietly at the table while the rest of us partied and laughed after our shows.

On this particular tour, Mats was the only Swedish musician on the roster. After a few drinks one night we asked Mats to teach us some Swedish. Mats stopped for a minute and said the phrase *suga min kok*. We tried to pronounce it and he repeated it many times so we all could get it correctly and burned into our brain. After we had the phrase down we asked him what it meant. We had no clue. Nice to see you? What time is it? Where is the bus? May I have a beer? We had no idea. He just said, "When you meet a Swedish person, tell them that."

For the next several days anytime I met a Swedish person I used the phrase. Much to my dismay I usually got a look of horror and disgust followed by the person turning and walking away without a word. It was a few nights later, drinking with another Swedish musician friend, that I learned *suga min kok* meant "suck my cock" in Swedish. Anytime I speak with Mats, I still say that phrase to him and we have a good laugh. He got us. The young pup pulled one over on the old dogs.

The first time I was in Sweden it didn't take me long to learn the Swedish word for kiss, but I was definitely taken aback. I don't remember exactly how it happened. But I do remember a Swedish girl saying the phrase to me *pus, pus*. I had no idea what that meant in Swedish but I immediately answered, *Yes, yes please*. I was thinking, *Wow, these European girls are really straight forward with sex*. Then she told me the Swedish word *pus* meant "kiss." Oh well, wishful thinking.

Another word that sticks out in my mind is the Danish word *Myrepatter*. One chilly night I had goosebumps and remarked to a woman how cold I was. I said I have goosebumps. She replied, *Myrepatter*. When I asked what that meant in Danish, she told me "ants' tits." I laughed and thought it was awesome. Nowadays when I get cold I don't get goosebumps I get ants' tits.

Another one of my tours took me to Gothenburg, Sweden, a small industrial shipping town on the west coast. There was a cruise ship that sailed to Norway, then to England on a three day cruise. In my hometown we had a factory called SKF. As kids we all called it the spoons, knives and forks factory. We knew that they actually made ball bearings and the company was owned by people from Sweden, but we still called it the spoons, knives and forks. When I first arrived in Gothenburg, on the taxi ride to the ship I passed an SKF factory. Thinking back to my childhood, I had never seen another SKF factory before and remembered they were from Sweden.

Later that night during a break at my show on the ship, I got to talking with a lovely Swedish lady who was kind of shy to speak with me in English. (I find this common when I'm in countries where English is not the native tongue.) We were struggling through a simple conversation, when she asked me if I knew any Swedish. I replied *no*. She asked me if I would like to learn some. I asked, *What does SKF stand for?* She replied, *Svenska Kullager Fabriken*, which in Swedish means Swedish ball bearing fabrication. Now it all made sense. I had a little trouble with the word *Kullager*, but after a few times she made sure I knew how to pronounce it correctly. I asked her if she had anything she wanted to learn in English.

She wanted to know what is the common slang word used for penis in American English. Now that's a big question. There are a lot of words used in American English, but I said probably "dick" is the most common. She repeated "dick", I repeated *Kullager* and off she bopped into the crowd and I went back to play my show.

The next evening, while on break, I was talking with a lovely older American couple, when I saw the same lady come bouncing through the pub. As she whizzed by I knew she meant to be pleasant and friendly with a phrase like "what's up?" She just looked at me and said, "Hey, how is your dick?" She just kept walking. The look on the face of the older couple was in complete disbelief and I was horrified.

On the same cruise ship, we had show dancers from England who perform nightly in the main show club. Since this was my first trip on a boat, after the show we all gathered in the Crew Lounge to have a drink and unwind. It was my first crew party. I've seen many since, and some were legendary! As the new guy, I sat quietly on a chair just listening to others talk while trying to fit in. As we drank, the girls chatting in their lovely British accent, a new dancer walked in and began to sit down. Quite loudly one of the other dancing girls exclaimed, "STOP! You don't want a dirty fag up your ass do you?" I spit beer through my nose. I'd forgotten the English refer to cigarettes as *fags*. (Funny, how two countries who speak the same language, words can still get confusing.) There was an ashtray on the seat and she was about to sit on it. They all looked at me to see if I was okay. I coughed and said, *I am fine, thank you, but what you just said means something totally different in my country and I don't want one either.* We all laughed and kept drinking.

Years ago I was leaving Sweden to go play a show in Oslo, Norway. I had very little money and my agent booked me on the cheapest bus to Norway at 6 p.m. I arrived at the station with my belongings, found the bus, stopped short and stared at the sign on the front of the bus. It said *sex bus*. In my mind I was thinking, *I know I told my agent to put me on the cheapest bus, but what the hell kind of kinky, sex-orgy bus is this?* I stood outside and watched the other passengers enter with horror. They were not the kind of people I wanted to be on a bus with, let alone see them naked and sweaty in carnal positions. There were old and crazy people of all shapes and kinds. I kept thinking, *I really need to get to this gig, but I'm not sure if I want to go this way?* I was considering trying to switch my ticket to another bus when the driver asked me if I was getting on the bus or not. I looked at him and said very suspiciously, *I think so. Is this the bus to Oslo?* He answered, "Yes, the six o'clock bus. That's what it says on the front." That's when I found out *sex* in Swedish means the number "six." I boarded the bus and set off for Oslo, nothing happened. Thank God!

I met another great, young Greek musician in Copenhagen named John. As we got to know each other I mentioned how I spent my honeymoon in Greece and how much I loved the people and their culture. He asked me if I spoke any Greek? I answered him, *Other than thank you and cheers, no.* He taught me the phrase *para moo tsibooki* and told me it meant "Hello do you speak Greek?" It really meant, "How about a blowjob." Dammit! Awkwardly, I got burned again, but I got him back. Anytime we would ride on a subway or a bus together I would yell loudly, *Hey, stop grabbing my ass. I am not going to have sex with you, I am straight.* He hated that.

My whole life I've always heard of them and referred to them as "pics." (Guitar picks) In Europe they call them *plectrums*. Something we American English speakers never understood. One night a friend of mine from Wales was playing a gig when he "bounced a pic." It's a common term referring to when you hit a string and the pick slips out of your fingers and goes flying through the darkness off the stage into the abyss. It happens to all of us.

On this particular night, he had only one pic when it went flying toward a cute little couple having drinks at a nearby table. Like the pro he is, he finished the song and took a short break to retrieve his pic. He walked over to the table, got down on his hands and knees and began to look for his guitar pic. When the young couple asked what he was doing under their table, he politely replied, "I have lost my pic. I'm sure it's under here somewhere and I need it. It's the only one I have and as soon as I find it I will be on my way. No worries." The couple looked at him in horror as he kept searching. Only later that night did he find out the word *pick* in Danish means "dick."

Along the same idea, another American musician friend of mine was playing in Denmark when he was talking with a few bar patrons about music. He is a talented and well-educated guitar player as I have met and can play anything. He was explaining to the folks that he should have been playing better, but he forgot his regular pic at home. All he had with him was this flimsy one. He preferred a much harder one, but this was the best he had at the moment. He then proceeded to tell them that he usually keeps a big blue one in his mouth as a backup just in case, but tonight he forgot it. The good news was, a friend of his was stopping by to bring him a bigger one later. You can't make this shit up.

I walked into a coffee shop to buy a cup of coffee and get rid of my Danish coins that I could not exchange. As the man behind the counter told me the total, I pulled a wad out of change out of my pocket and spread it on the counter for him to count. I noticed among the change there were a few guitar pics. Not thinking I blurted out, *I am sorry, I always have a bunch of pics in my pocket mixed in with my money.* He just looked at me and snickered, I knew what I had done.

Myrtle Beach, South Carolina 1992.

Charlie's Nightlife, Murrells Inlet, South Carolina 1994.

Nashville show 1998.

Ubu and I taking a nap, Nashville Tennessee.

My Dad on stage at The Grand Ole Opry, Nashville Tennessee.

Myself and Randy Mallory, Nashville1999.

The Musician Flat in Copenhagen Denmark along with Richie Campbell, Myself, Gary Owen, Ken Gulbreath and Duncan Gillies, 2001.

Musicians Flat, Copenhagen 2000.

Andy McDonald, Copenhagen 2000.

Myself and Mick Hutchinson, Copenhagen 2002.

Musician Flat, Copenhagen 2001.

Myself with the English Dance Girls aboard The M/s Princess of Scandinavia, Sweden 2001.

Cruise Ship Band and Cruise Manager aboard the M/s Gabriella, Sweden 2002.

Love God

Sometimes you just have to call someone out. Meaning you just can't say something and not show proof. I refer to that as *get your dick out,* not literally, just meaning get your dick out on the table and prove it's just as big or bigger than everyone else, don't just talk to talk. I've said that phrase for years and it has always been a figure of speech until one night in Copenhagen.

After the show I was sitting around the table with a bunch of other musicians as we usually did; chilling, drinking, smoking and talking. We were unwinding from another night of *fabulous stardom.* We were chatting about the usual crap music, people we had met in the bars, girls and stupid things we had done in our lives.

Somewhere along the night we got to talking about tattoos. One of the guys at the table was from Scotland. (This will make you so proud as a country.) He announced he got so drunk one night he got a tattoo on his penis saying Love God and didn't remember it until the next morning when he woke up and found it. Hold on now. I have heard stories about people being drunk and getting tattoos they don't remember. Ironically, I have another friend that same thing happened to in Thailand. She got a tattoo on her head behind her ear and had no memory of it until the next day when she woke and her head hurt. She looked in the mirror and she noticed she was missing hair and had a tattoo behind her ear. It can happen.

Let me preface what happened next by saying as far as I know all of us male musicians we're straight to my knowledge, but when you make a statement like that you got to get your dick out, and he did. Son of a b**** he was not lying. There it was poorly tattooed in writing "Love God."

This brings up so many unanswered questions.

The obvious question - how drunk do you have to be not to remember that? Someone with a needle drawing on your member! What the fuck? Apparently he had been on a binge fueled by alcohol and "other substances" for days prior to the artwork. Let's just say I myself was not impressed with the quality of work, but glad he told the truth. Also glad it wasn't me. It was a horrible tattoo.

After seeing his "Mini Me" I got to thinking about the age-old question every musician gets often and just hates: the first time you are with someone and they turn to you and say, "You're a musician, I bet you do this with a different girl every night." There it is. I hate that question. Then comes the delicate, potentially deal-breaking reply, *actually no*, and see if she believes you? It's always awkward and no matter what your answer is they still have doubt.

Let me tell you a secret about being a musician. Most of the time they are telling the truth when they say "no." Being a musician has its perks. There are a lot of ass-chasing musicians sluts out there who give us all a bad name. Refer to the "One Bad Apple" saying. I'm not saying that in my single days I did not have my lucky streaks, but there were way more dry spells. If you're a big-name star, the opportunity comes way more often than the average Joe. Eventually the reality of one-night stands and trying to remember their names just gets old and fades away.

The cold hard truth is as a musician I have seen way more bartenders, waitresses, patrons, security guards and ugly bastards get laid than me. They were all working their magic while I was on stage setting the mood like a soundtrack to their pornos. When the time comes that the musician finishes the show, it's late and there's not much left in the bar except the sound of trash cans and the clinking of beer bottles being thrown away by the staff.

Everyone is already gone on their merry way and you are left hot and sweaty to clean up your gear, have a drink and try to unwind and go home alone. That's the truth. That's why all of us musicians were sitting around the table that night looking at the other guy's penis anyway.

After seeing his tattoo, I kind of felt bad for him. I personally believe that tattoos are meant to be seen, but that one was tough. How awkward it must be to be with a girl for the first time and when she asks the inevitable question oh, you reply no and then produce that like a billboard on your penis. It just has to be weird Time After Time.

After that I made a promise to myself to never get a tattoo while drinking. What seems like a good idea at the time may come back to haunt you later. Drunken tattoos do happen all the time. It's not an urban myth, sadly I have seen it.

Uh Oh

The human body is a funny thing. It's YOUR body, but YOU can't control IT. It does what it wants during your whole lifetime.

Every job has its dangers - those *Oh, shit* moments that we all don't see coming. As one man on stage alone, my job has those moments. Over the years I have learned to hold my bladder as long as I can on stage. At one point in my career I was so trained with my urine routine I only pissed every four hours even off stage. Every four hours like clockwork in the day or the middle of the night, I went to the bathroom and let out a stream like a pregnant camel. It was weird; my body got conditioned like *Pavlov's dogs*. Nowadays, I just can't hold that long anymore and it's also dangerous.

This is one of the reasons I don't drink beer on stage anymore. First of all it makes you pee a lot and once you have broken the seal it's all over. I also don't drink it because it makes me feel bloated, lazy and belch a lot. The visual stimulation of watching people in the audience walk past you to piss all the time is tough as well. I try not to think about it and just keep playing.

I have heard many horror stories about some guys pissing themselves on stage. A guitar player friend pissed himself on stage one night and took a water bottle and poured it all over his head like a sweaty *rockstar*. Water covered his shirt, body and pants. In all actuality it was to cover up the big wet pee spot in the front of his jeans. A smart move, but also very dangerous since he was playing an electric guitar.

My friend Jared Michael Hobgood, used to piss himself on stage just for the *shock value.* I saw it more than once. He would INTENTIONALLY wear light-colored khaki pants so the audience could see the spot in his pants grow down his leg. He would sit on stage and tell the audience "Gimme a minute, I have to pee." He would just sit there and let go without ever moving from the stool. The audience reaction was a complete shock and he loved every minute of it and he just laughed.

I myself have pissed my pants on stage. One night at *Irish Kevin's* I was in the last song of my show. I had to go real bad, but thought I could hold it until I finished. Wrong. My bladder was holding like The Hoover Dam. I said my farewell and hit the final last high note. Just then I felt my bladder let go. I quickly turned around on stage and finished the last note of the song with my back to the audience, at the same time there was a stream of piss running down my leg and soaking my jeans. The security guards and next act looked at me like "what are you doing just standing there?" That's when they noticed the large wet spot growing in my jeans. We laughed hysterically and I even had to get a mop to clean up the stage before the next Act. The audience never knew a thing. I got away with it. There is still a picture of me taken by Little Brian, one of the security guards. He snapped a picture backstage with me in piss-soaked jeans, just laughing. What can I say - you can't stop in mid-stream.

Even worse is being on stage and getting the gut bubbles. Yep, that moment when you realize your body tells you have to go now! Uh oh!

I have carried Imodium onstage with me for years for just that reason. All musicians have had this happen to them. It's easier with a duo or a band because you can have the others cover for you while you run to the bathroom. It happened to me a few years before when I was playing in a band. I just had the other guys sing a few songs until I could make it back to the stage. No one was any the wiser.

One year, during *Fantasy Fest* in Key West, was different. I was dressed in costume on stage and playing my normal show. The stomach flu had been going around and I knew a few people had it earlier in the week. I was on stage doing my thing and all was fine until about two hours into the show. It hit me like a freight train. I immediately got the chills and the cold sweats. My stomach was cramping like crazy and the vibration from my guitar resting on my belly was not helping. Neither were the high notes I had to hit by pushing with my diaphragm. I popped an Imodium, but it was too late. I held it as long as I could and finally had to excuse myself to go to the bathroom. It was not pretty. I rushed and hurried the best I could to get back onstage so people thought I was pissing. I had two hours left on stage during our busiest week of the year. I downed another Imodium and started singing again. Five minutes later I had to make another run for the bathroom. I had cold sweats, I was holding my ass cheeks together like a bank vault and trying not to move for fear of shitting myself on stage. I had to readjust my guitar and rest it on my hip bone instead of my stomach, but it didn't help much with the vibration still shooting through my body. I spent the next two hours running to the bathroom every fifteen minutes. It was horrible and I was so scared I was going to shit myself and it would be all over the Internet. The bar staff kept looking at me like what the hell is going on? They knew something was up. Thankfully, I finished without a stage incident and went home. I spent the next thirty-six hours in the bathroom. I also had taken three Imoduims in two hours on stage that day, so after the flu was gone I didn't shit for days. Several other people got the same stomach flu the next few weeks.

From the audience perspective, what musicians do on stage may look easy. You don't often think of things we go through without others knowing. No matter what you do for a living, all I can say is sometimes your job is just shitty.

Strange Things Happen On A Boat

You see strange things when you work on a cruise ship. I have seen a lot of strange things happen to others and myself. To the best of my memories these are few that stick out.

One summer night, while working a cruise ship from Helsinki to Stockholm, I was playing the first set of the night. The sun was still up and most of the people we're still outside on the upper decks enjoying the scenery and warm weather. I say upper decks because there were three open decks directly above me and the rest, including the deck I was on, were enclosed.

I was facing a long row of windows across the bar as I was quietly playing "cocktail music" when a body went flying past the window in a downward motion. After all the times I have played this gig, that was a first. I immediately knew someone had gone overboard. I didn't know if they fell or if they jumped, but someone was on the express lane to the water. I turned to the bartender to tell her what I had just seen, she saw it too. She reached for the phone and when the alarms went off the ship abruptly stopped. I still don't know what happened that evening. I don't know how it happened or if they ever found that person. All I know was I kept playing, and not long after, the boat continued on its merry way.

Another night after my gig I was cleaning up my gear when I heard a ruckus in the hall across from the bar. I noticed a guy pushing two naked men down the hallway on a luggage cart, yelling and screaming as they laughed. They sped past me and I assumed they were passengers who had too much to drink and shortly thereafter would be stopped by security. I never saw them again. I found out the next day they were not passengers; it was the crew doing beer luggage races.

Another time, I was sitting on stage when a gypsy man approached me and told me he wanted to play my guitar and sing. I told him that was against the rules, I was there to sing. He suddenly produced a knife and said, "Give me your guitar or I'm going to cut you." I replied, *You have a better chance of seeing Jesus walk in than you do getting my guitar.* I am very protective of her. The bar staff saw him do it, called security immediately and they threw the guy in "boat jail." Yes, there is a jail on cruise ships. He spent the rest of his voyage locked up before being turned over to the police at the next port.

Some European people have a funny way of celebrating bachelor parties. It's much different from the American bachelor party. Instead of strippers and alcohol, their peers dress up their bachelor friend in awful woman's clothing and they all get stupid drunk. There is also a difference in my opinion to "American Drunk" and "European Drunk." If you have had too much to drink in the United States, most of the time they will cut you off. From what I have seen in Europe, it's not that way. If you are still upright and conscious you can have another drink. We all know people drinking do stupid things.

One particular night, I was working when we got word that there were a group of *Hell's Angels* on board. I don't have any problems with bikers, but the crew and security were all on full alert. There was also a bachelor party on board and they were dressed like superheroes. The bachelor party boys were already drunk when they arrived on the boat and continued drinking as the cruise went on. My pub was full of *Hells Angels* who were drinking and not bothering anyone. At some point, one of the superheroes bumped a biker and spilled his beer. It was on! Full blast! It was like a scene from the old Batman TV show. Zonk! Pow! Wham! I turned my back to the audience to protect my guitar, as glasses and chairs were flying. There was a full brawl going on in the pub - Bikers vs. Superheroes. I kept an eye over my shoulder just to make sure I wasn't hit by anything or anyone. The Bikers were beating the shit out of the Superheroes. At one point a big fat biker was sitting on Superman's chest, slamming his head against the floor. I remember thinking, *Wow, Superman is getting his ass kicked, this doesn't look good for The Hall of Justice.* After a few minutes, security finally arrived to break it up. The bar was a total mess. There was spilled booze and broken glass everywhere. Turned-over chairs and superheroes were sprawled out in the aftermath. It was the best fight I have ever seen and I must say the bikers won that one. I got the rest of the night off after that. The next morning the bikers got off the boat and left. I did, however, see some of the Superheroes again the next night. They were not in costume anymore, but they were easy to spot with their black eyes and bruises. I am pretty sure they were all hungover as well.

On one of the cruises, I took my drummer, Tom, along with me. We were playing a packed bar with standing-room only. Without any provocation, a drunk guy standing in front of the stage threw a whole glass of vodka soda on me and my guitar. In the middle of rocking out I stopped immediately. Tom trailed off for a beat or two, noticing I had stopped without warning. He knew something was wrong. I turned to him and said, *We're taking a break* and took my guitar off. I am normally a very mild-mannered, easy-going guy, it takes A LOT to get me mad, but when you do, look out! This guy just threw a drink on me and I never said a word to him.

As Tom and I both remember it, I walked off stage and grabbed the guy by the throat. I drug him across the pub in front of the whole audience we were just playing for. The audience and his friends watched in horror as I slammed him against the wall, holding him in a death grip. I held him up so his toes could barely touch the floor. I was on a complete adrenaline high and fuming mad. The bartender looked at me in shock when I uttered the phrase *call security now*. His friends tried to calm me down and told me he was drunk and didn't mean it. They would buy me a drink if I just let him go and forget it. No fucking way! He just threw a sticky booze and soda not only all over me, but my guitar and gear. That stuff can ruin electronics. Security came and I released him from my grip. They marched him off to "boat jail." I turned to the bartender and said, *We're taking a break*. I motioned to Tom and he followed me out of the bar and down to my cabin. The entire audience was in full silence and disbelief of what just happened. We returned to my cabin and poured ourselves a big drink of Jack Daniels and tried to calm down. Tom remarked, "Holy Shit! I have never seen that side of you. I knew you were pissed, but that was awesome!" After an extended break we returned to the bar to finish the show. Much to our surprise, the bar was still full of people waiting for us to go back to playing. However, when we walked in the crowd suddenly went silent. You could have heard a mouse fart. I guess they figured because we were Americans, we probably had guns. Ha ha, not the case. We got back on stage and I apologized for the sudden interruption. The crowd applauded and we continued to rock out the rest of the show.

Out of all the things that have happened to be on a boat over the years, the best thing that ever happened to me was I met my future wife. In the summer of 2002, I was working on a ship from Helsinki to Stockholm. My wife-to-be had just returned to Helsinki after living and working in South Africa for six months. Two of her girlfriends decided to take her on a cruise as a welcome home gift. I had never met any of them before, but I watched them come in and out of the bar. I was playing all night long, while they bopped around the boat on their "girls trip." I ended my show, cleaned up my gear and headed to the boat's *discotek* for a drink. It was the only late night place open on the boat. Outside the disco, I spotted the three girls that I had seen earlier. Still in my stage clothes, one of them said, "Hey aren't you the Troubadour?" I replied, *Yes*! We began chatting and that is the night I met Hannah, Pia and Marika. We talked for a while before someone mentioned playing the game Truth or Dare. I am in! Three hot Finnish girls, and I am single on a boat in the middle of the Baltic Sea! We played for a while, but nothing ever happened before we returned to our cabins for the night. The next day they were headed back to Helsinki and they would be gone.

The next day they got off the boat and I flew out to play a month-long gig in Oslo, Norway. I had been on the road for five months in a row and I was skinny and tired. I never saw any of them again until six months later. We kept in touch through email and I began talking with Marika. When I returned to Copenhagen for a New Year's Eve show she came to visit me.

It had been six months since we had seen each other face-to-face. That was before either of us had Skype. When she arrived at the Copenhagen airport she was worried she would not recognize me. I met her like I promised I would. What she didn't know was my humorous side. I have a set of false movie teeth I have had for years that a friend gave me for Christmas. They are absolutely hideous! The actual name of the model of teeth I have is "Incest." Teeth going every direction, gum sores and all. I love them. I wear them every time I get a chance just to see people's reaction. When I met her at the airport, I had them in and she had no idea.

I tapped her on the shoulder and she turned around. Her eyes got as big as tea saucers as she met me face-to-face. As she tells it, she didn't know if I was in a horrible accident or was she drunk when she met me. But she didn't remember me looking like this. Her plan was she was going to be polite and stay for the night, but the next day she was gone. I kept those false teeth in all the way through the airport and into the taxi on our way back to the flat. She couldn't even look at me and I was having a blast trying to keep a straight face. After about twenty minutes in the cab and much to her delight, I took out the false teeth and revealed the prank. I guess she was pleased?

We had our first date on New Year's Eve 2003. She admitted to me that when she first met me she didn't like me at all. She thought I was a rude, egotistical American asshole. (*How did that work out for ya?*) Eventually her opinion changed and we continued dating over the next year or so until we were married in July of 2004.

On our first Valentine's Day together I bought her very own fake redneck false teeth. We wore them into our wedding reception to meet the crowd the day we got married.

Big Jon

It was summertime in Scandinavia. I was performing on a cruise ship from Stockholm, Sweden to Helsinki, Finland. A lot of passengers who travel there this time of year are Scandinavians on their way to their "summer cottage," family reunions, holiday or some kind of music festival. It's a busy time of year and the boats are full to capacity.

I was working on the ship when I got a knock at my cabin door before the show. It was the Cruise Manager just informing me that we had *Hells Angels* aboard that night. Now I have no problem with bikers, hell, I am one myself, and they are some of the sweetest, most giving, kind people in the world. For the most part if you don't cross them you are fine. As long as you treat the bikers with respect and kindness you are good.

I've seen documentaries about how the *Hell's Angels* are alive and well. Most of the time in the United States we don't hear much about them on the news anymore like we did back in the 60's and 70's. I assume they are doing "their business" and I don't want to know. I can tell you that the *Hell's Angels* in Scandinavia are alive and well. From my experience there is a lot more public activity, attention and trouble on that side of the pond. I've seen it on the news and in the papers many times abroad. When my Cruise Manager told me they were on board, *I Was Not Afraid*, just on alert.

There were no metal detectors in port security prior to boarding this ship. I had heard rumors they had guns and knives and I did not want to see any of them. I had already had a knife pulled on me by a gypsy man one night on the same ship who wanted to play my guitar. He never played her and went to "boat jail" for the rest of his cruise. That night with the *Hell's Angels* I had my eyes and ears open.

As I walked into the bar for my show, I saw it was full of *Hell's Angels*. Black clothing, leather patches, tattoos, bandanas, long hair, beards and the whole nine yards. There must have been thirty of them taking up most of the tables. The man closest to me on stage sat with his back to me as I began to set up for my show. In black letters across the back of his shirt it said "Support Your Local *Al-Qaeda.*"

I stopped and looked at his shirt and said to myself, *SHIT, I am American and they are going to hate me.*

I began my show, played my first song, in English, finished it, then spoke every bit of Finnish language I knew at the time. I didn't know much - *Good evening, Hello, Welcome and Drink.* I was hoping to ease the tension that might be in the room. The guy in front of me, a mountain of a man, got up and walked right over to the stage in front of me. Just for the record, he was about six foot seven or six foot eight, easily 350 pounds, wide as a truck, and mean looking. He had a long, full beard, was bald, and missing his right eye. Yes, I said, *missing an eye.* There was no glass eye replacement, just one eyelid sewn shut and he was enormous.

I politely looked up at him. He was taller than me even though I was on stage. I spoke, *Good evening. What can I do for you? Do you have a request?* He glared down at me and put fifty Swedish Kronor in my tip jar. (About five bucks.) He simply said these words that made my body shutter: "Shut up, we are trying to drink here." Inside, my heart dropped, fear came over my little shaking legs and I just looked at him. In my head I was thinking to myself, *You know Jeff, you can die any day. And today is as good a day as any. Think of the great headline that will make, "Musician Jeff Harris killed by Scandinavian One-Eyed Sasquatch Biker."*

With fear in my body, I looked into my tip jar, looked backed up at him and said, *If you want me to shut up, you're going to have to give me a lot more fucking money than that!* I stared at him and waited for the impending doom. He never flinched, with a straight face and an intimidating tone said, "You drink?" I replied, *Jack Daniels, straight up.* He held up one finger and headed for the bar. The crowd parted like Moses in the Red Sea as I just stood there. He returned in about ten seconds with a double shot of Jack. The fastest bar service I have ever seen in Scandinavia. He handed me the drink, I looked at him and his "one eye" and shot the whole thing down. I handed the glass back to him and said, *Don't you ever bring me an empty glass again.* He smiled and said, "I like you." I said, *What is your name?* He replied, "Big Jon" (pronounced like yawn) in Scandinavia. I said, *I am Jeff,* and extended my hand for a shake.

He responded with a shake, bought me another drink and sat back down. He and the rest of *The Angels* watched me for the rest of the night. Anytime anyone approached the stage to tip me or ask for a song request, he watched them like a one-eyed hawk and was ready at any moment to protect his little American, elf friend. I would just wink at him - no pun intended. I would smile and politely give him a wave to let him know all was okay, I didn't need any help.

Following the show, Big Jon and I went to the late night bar on the boat, the only thing open. We proceeded to drink and chat in broken English until the bar closed. If anyone came near me or wanted to talk to me, or shake my hand saying "nice show" they had to get through Big Jon first. He towered over me and protected me the rest of the night. He even followed me into the bathroom when I had to pee to make sure no one fucked with me. In hind-sight, that could have been an ugly story because at this point I'm pretty sure I was the bitch in this relationship. He was a gentleman, and made sure no one messed with me.

When the bar closed, we walked back through the corridor where the secure "crew area" was, we shook hands and bid goodnight. I wished him well and safe travels. He remarked he hoped to see me again sometime.

The next morning the boat pulled into Helsinki Harbor. I heard the rumble of Harleys in the bowels of the ship like thunder and then fade into the distance. I never saw Big Jon again, but every time I see a *Hell's Angels* patch or a *one-eyed* man I think of him.

Halloween With The Russians

It was October when I was playing on a cruise ship in Scandinavia. This particular ship was the newest, most prestigious, state-of-the-art flagship for the cruise line and this gig was big. This particular ship only cruised for twenty hours, it was a party ship. Passengers boarded in the early evening and we set sail at 7 p.m. We went basically nowhere, just sailed in circles around the Baltic Sea all night until we went back to the port about 4 p.m. the next day. The only purpose of this cruise was for passengers to buy tax-free alcohol and get drunk, wild and laid. It was that simple, some of us crew referred to it as the "Shag Ship." People got crazy aboard that massive boat. Each day we would watch all the passengers leave the gangway still hungover, drunk or stumbling back to the terminal. When you say discount alcohol to a Scandinavian it's like Christmas.

I worked in the pub in the front of the ship near the disco. Some of my friends were in the band and worked in the main showroom upstairs on the eleventh deck. This main showroom also had a dance show, and on this particular trip, we had three Russian circus acrobats doing a special feature show. I watched them rehearse. Two guys held a long balance beam between their shoulders and a third guy would flip around high in the air like a monkey. It was very cool to watch, but I didn't want to do it.

I have been to many "crew parties" on ships before. For those of you reading this, "crew parties" are fun, some are legendary. As a passenger you don't even know they happen. When the crew gets done with work for the day, just like everyone else, they want to drink and unwind. We crew all lived in the same areas of the ship, next door to each other. You just line up down a long hallway that the passengers have no access to. There are secret doors in some of the ships with electronic codes that the passengers can't access. Sometimes the crew are within one foot of the passengers, just on the other side of the wall, and they have no idea.

When you work on a cruise ship for weeks or months on end, life gets a little boring and monotonous. The best way to pass the time is by passing a bottle up and down the hallway and just hanging out. It happens more times than you think. I feel it is important to mention that the people in charge of navigating the ship are NOT involved. The Captain and his Bridge Crew along with Security are completely sober, and in close attention to safety and the job at hand. However, there is a good chance that your waiter, bartender, band, dancers and gift shop employees are getting hammered. If your waiter at breakfast smells like alcohol, looks like they haven't slept and is wearing two different shoes, they might have been at a crew party the night before. I have personally seen it happen, an employee wearing two different shoes.

I have been to many crew parties over the years but the best one I ever went to happened on Halloween. Following our shows that night at about 2 a.m., we gathered outside our rooms in the common area and began to drink hard. I, along with the band, the dancers, the Russians, the DJs, the magician and some of the other crew participated.

A crowd of this size had some dangerous potential and definitely way too much alcohol readily available. Each of us produced a bottle, or beer from our rooms and we were off. We drank for a while with music blaring, followed by a brief trip to the crew sauna. One guy actually cooked sausage over the coals in the sauna and actually burned his hand badly. At this point no one cared and we just kept drinking. We left the sauna and returned to the common area outside our rooms and kept going with the party.

That night I learned a very strange Russian tradition I will still do occasionally when I meet someone from Russia. Igor, the head of the circus performers, was a nice, older man from Kiev. He taught me that in Russia when they drink Vodka you do four things. First, take a big inhale of a breath and then exhale. Next, take a big full-cheek gulp of vodka, then smell your own armpit or the top of the head of the person next to you, finally, swallow the vodka. I know it's a weird thing to do, but we continued to do it all night long. The Russians know their vodka.

Somewhere in the middle of the mayhem someone mentioned it was Halloween. Europeans are not as big into Halloween as Americans are. No trick or treat for candy, but we had beer and we decided to dress up for the holiday using costumes from the Dancers' Closet. We all looked through the closet, picked out our costume and returned to our cabins to change for the reveal. The costume options were limited so we did our best. I found an old Russian Military Officer's dress jacket. I wore my American flag sweatpants and a sombrero. I went as the United Nations. We also had an Indian, a bunny, a hippie, one of the band members dressed in a fairy costume and finally, the lead guitar player was Santa Claus. We laughed and kept drinking for hours. Every once in a while one of the security guards would pass through on his routine check and laugh at us and each time we were more drunk and now wearing costumes.

One of the cleaning people left a cart full of towels in the corner of the common room. I'm not sure who started it, but at some point someone started a massive towel fight. There were towels everywhere, dirty towels not real hygienic, in hindsight.

About 7 a.m. we were still going strong when someone mentioned we should get something to eat in the Crew Mess. I am sure we were all totally intoxicated at this point. We made our way down the hallways and finally arrived at the door of the Mess. Santa opened the door and fell flat on his face right in front of the ship's Captain. He was eating breakfast and saw all of us drunk and dressed in costume. He was not pleased, to say the least. We decided a quick retreat back to our cabins and off to bed was the best idea.

With the common area still trashed with beer cans, empty wine and vodka bottles, costumes and towels scattered about the room, we all went to pass out. About an hour later we were all woken by a loud knock on our cabin doors. It was the Cruise Manager. We all gathered in the common areas still wobbly and blurry-eyed when he reprimanded all of us and told us to clean this up immediately. He was pissed! The dancers lived in a different hallway along with the Russians, so they were not subjected to the evidence. Just the band and me.

We cleaned up the mess, returned the costumes, and went back to bed. The next night none of us felt well and we went to bed early. We all laughed about the look on the Captain's face when Santa fell through the door. Oops, Merry Christmas or Happy Halloween?

I never worked that ship again after that or the band. We got blackballed from that ship. I'm not sure if it was the Captain or the Cruise Manager? My agent later asked me about the party. I simply replied, *What party?* Word of the party had gotten back to him, but I didn't care. I didn't really care for the staff on that ship anyway. They were not friendly to the entertainers and besides, after that night there was no way we could top that party. It was one for the record books.

I still have my Russian Military Officer's jacket.

Meg Ryan

What can I say? We all have that "top three list." The top three people in this world that if we get a chance to have sex with anyone on that list, we get a free hall pass from our significant other with no questions asked. My top three are Marilyn Monroe, Cameron Diaz and Meg Ryan, with a substitute of Angelina Jolie, because Marilyn Monroe is dead. The chance of me meeting, let alone having the option to be intimate with any of them is almost non-existent, but there is still a chance. I almost had that happen one night in Oslo, Norway.

I was playing a gig at a fish house/bar called *Rorbua*. It was a quaint little place right on the dock of the Oslo Harbor and it was summertime. The pier was crowded with lots of folks, tourists and locals alike enjoying the big boats and the sights and sounds of the beautiful warm summer weather. I was playing my gig, minding my own business, when a young lady sitting at a table nearby caught my eye. She had short blonde, curly hair, a denim mini skirt, a cute little red and white checkered top and high heels. As I continued to play, she eventually turned around so that I could see her face and my heart dropped, *Holy shit, it's Meg Ryan!*

This girl looks exactly like Meg Ryan. In my mind I was thinking, *Is this her?* At the time Meg Ryan was still making movies and it is not uncommon for big Hollywood movie stars to be in Europe shooting a movie on site, and could this be her? Maybe she is just happy to see another American like I usually am when I am on tour abroad. During the rest of my set we began to make eye contact and she was smiling at me. Bingo! This is a good thing. She was sitting with a bunch of other men and women, but she was definitely checking me out, and I was her. I liked her great legs coming out of that mini skirt and it was working for me. When I finished my last set for the night it was still early. I began to pack up my guitar when I felt a tap on my shoulder. I turned around and it was Meg. Like a nervous little school boy I smiled and said hello. She spoke in broken English, said I was very good and she liked my music, would I like to join her for a drink? And I said yes. At this time I immediately realized that this was not the real Meg Ryan, but her Norwegian doppelganger. I didn't care! She told me her name, which I can't remember. It didn't matter for the rest of the night she was still Meg Ryan and I was going to do my damnedest to be Dennis Quaid. She and her friends decided to go to a nearby place called *The Beer Palace*, a bar not far away where the bar staff and I would go after work to have a drink and unwind.

All was going well. I was sitting at a long wooden table of about eight Norwegians, men and women, three on each side on wooden picnic benches, with one chair at each end. Meg was sitting on the end and me right beside her. For a while Meg and I were talking and there was conversation going around the table in Norwegian. I didn't understand and I didn't care. It's a normal thing to me when I am on tour abroad to have conversations going on around me in *Ooogly boogly* language. Oblivion is a beautiful thing. After a while Meg and I were still talking and things were going in the right direction. I excused myself to go to the men's room.

When I walked out of the men's room Meg was there waiting for me to exit. She kissed me and said, "You have tattoos." As she looked at my arm, she said, "I have a tattoo also, do you want to see it?" Stupid question. *Hell yeah!* She took my hand, pulled me into a single bathroom stall and locked the door. It was then that I knew I was about to be Dennis Quaid. *I am about to bang Meg Ryan!* At least in my mind she was. She bent over the toilet and lifted her mini skirt over her perfect little Norwegian ass. She had nothing on underneath that tight little skirt. She hoisted it up high over her hips and showed me her tattoo. She had a tramp stamp on her lower back. *Wow that's a nice one,* was all I could say. Then she asked me if I wanted to come home with her for the night. She said her apartment was a few blocks away and she would like it if I did. Let me think? *Yes, yes, yes.* I am about to be Dennis Quaid. I am about to bang Meg Ryan. Not literally, but I was pretending she was. I was in. The deal was sealed and it was just a matter of time before I put my checkmark next to one of my *top three.* She said, "All I have to do is go say goodbye to my friends and then we will go." I followed her back to the table, we sat down and finished what was left of our beers.

Meg took her seat; I sat down beside her where I was. Like a kid just before Christmas morning, filled with excitement, I killed what was left of my beer and beamed with anticipation while Meg was speaking to the others.

What happened next was in complete fast forward. In a matter of seconds, Meg finished what was left in her pint glass, shot up, tipping her chair over backward, yelled something in Norwegian and in one smooth move smashed her pint glass on the guy's forehead across the table from me. She made an about-face, turned and stormed away. I was in complete shock. There was yelling, glass and blood everywhere as I watched her walk out the door. It was a huge scene with everyone yelling and looking at me. I felt extremely uncomfortable and outnumbered. What just happened? They were speaking Norwegian. My buddy from the bar looked across the room at me "like what was that?" I just got up and left. I walked outside hoping to find Meg and get an explanation. It was too late. She disappeared into the Oslo night and I never saw her again. Till this day I still have no idea what happened? All I know is I was about to have sex with Meg Ryan and she left me high and dry in a cloud of shattered glass.

Anytime I watch a Meg Ryan movie I think of that night and it makes me sad.

Skirm

To my understanding the word "Skirm" is a short term used by Irish for the word skirmish, meaning a fight. To me, the word was a man's name.

I met Skirm in Oslo, Norway, in 2001 when he was the leader of a band playing in *The Dubliner, a* pub downstairs from where I lived. He was an extremely talented musician and his band was very popular and smokin' to say the least.

Skirm was the front man and a left-handed guitar player. He played a right-handed guitar upside down and it just messed with my brain to watch him play. It still does, and I think of him every time I see a left-handed guitar player slaying an axe upside down. It just completely confused me and every-thing I have ever learned on guitar. I get entranced and can't stop watching their hands. I went to see Skirm and his band play almost every night for the weeks they were in Oslo.

Prior to his arrival I had been in Oslo for a few weeks on a month-long gig. Like many other times early in my career, I had little or no money. We always got paid at the end of the gig and I always sent my money back home to my mom to pay bills. The deal with the bar was I played six nights a week, got two beers a night and a meal. The problem was I was playing in a fish house and anyone who knows me knows I don't eat fish or seafood of any kind. I like to go fishing, but I don't eat what I catch and the smell of fish makes me nauseous. It was a long, hungry, poor month to say the least.

Not only was I broke and hungry, but Norway is one of the most expen-sive countries I've ever been in. A pint of beer at that time was easily nine U.S. Dollars and a pack of cigarettes was about eleven bucks. I didn't make much in tips at the bar I was playing (which is common) in Norway so I needed another way to supplement my cash-on-hand problem. Each night after my gig finished at 11 p.m. I would pack up my guitar and make my way to the main walking street, *Johan Gate,* in the center of Oslo and "busk" on the street for an hour or two to make some extra money. My first time busking was the scariest show I have ever played.

I have played in front of crowds of thousands, played on stage with national artists, performed in front of record company executives, movie stars, world renowned sports figures and more, but I have never been more scared as I was that first time on *Johan Gate.*

The difference is, when I perform on stage I am in control of my surroundings for the most part. I am comfortable with the sound system, my equipment, the stage, the lights, and I know how to read my audience and know what they want. They are there to drink, listen to music and be entertained. It's a pretty simple equation, but when you are busking it is a totally different atmosphere.

Your audience is just a common person walking down the street, headed to another destination. You have to get their attention with your music and impress them enough to tip you in just a matter of seconds before they are gone. There is no warm-up or setting the mood. It's like throwing a musical grenade and hoping it hits someone.

My first night playing on the street I will never forget. I had seen many guys do it for years and never thought about how intimidating it was until I stopped and opened my case. I found a spot, put down my case and was getting ready to play when another Busker from about two blocks away came over and told me to move. According to him I was too close to him. Apparently these guys are very territorial.

I moved a few more blocks away, opened up my case and began to sing. The first ten minutes were the most self-doubting, nerve-wracking ten minutes I have ever played. I still remember thinking to myself, *God, I suck, I am horrible, no one is tipping me.* People just kept walking past me without even a glance. I was invisible to them. My guitar case was totally empty and I was feeling ashamed of myself when someone threw a small coin into my case. It was just a small coin, but to me it was like a million dollars and a reassurance that I was *not that bad.* I didn't make much money the first night, but I made enough to buy a pack of cigarettes and a beer.

On my way back to my flat I passed by the other Busker and noticed he had a case full of money. He was doing much better and I wondered why? At that point I could have jumped and robbed him, but I am not that kind of person. So I decided to figure out what he was doing that was different that made him successful. The next night, instead of busking, I went on a secret reconnaissance mission.

I strolled around the streets after my show without my case and looked like a normal walker. I checked out some of the other players. Some sang in English performing American, Irish or British songs and one or two of them sang in Norwegian. I took mental notes as I got to the guy that made me move the night before.

I walked past him, invisible, as he played *Proud Mary*. He had a few people watching him and his case was full as I kept walking. I turned the corner, walked around the block and stopped just behind the building so he couldn't see me. I watched and listened and learned his secret.

He would watch for people to approach him and just when they were about to get in earshot of him, he would start singing and playing again. He was playing *Proud Mary*. As the people passed by and got out of range he would stop playing. A minute or so later, he repeated the same thing. With each new passing person he sang the chorus to *Proud Mary*. If the crowd stopped, he kept playing the song, but if they moved on he stopped. I listened to him do this for about a half hour. Each time with *Proud Mary*, that's when I got it!

He just played one popular song that most of the people knew and loved. Actually, I think that was the only song he knew. Every time I passed him the rest of the month, he was playing *Proud Mary*. I don't even know if he knew the whole song or any other song at all. But it worked, and he was making money. The next time I set up to busk, I began to sing the chorus of *American Pie* as people approached me. It worked like a charm and the coins began to flow into my case like rain. I had played long enough each night to buy a pack of cigarettes, a beer and a little extra. I saved the extra coins for ten Kroner cheeseburger day at *McDonald's* every Thursday. I would walk in and order about twenty cheeseburgers. The staff looked at me like, "Fucking American," but I didn't care. I would eat one or two cheeseburgers and then put the rest in the fridge in the flat for the next few days. It may have not been the healthiest diet, but I needed to eat. That month I figured out how to busk and make a little side money. I was scraping by when I was introduced to Skirm.

He just went by Skirm. I don't remember his real name. He got that nickname when he was a kid because he used to get in fights at school and the name stuck. He was a tall man, over six feet and well built like a rugby player. He had a pale, freckled skin and red hair cut short into a crew cut. He was just a few years older than me and a lifelong musician.

I quickly learned Skirm, like many other musicians I know, had a playful, practical-joker, devious side. I learned early in our relationship that if he turned to me and silently raised his bushy eyebrows up and down, I was to just follow his lead. Whatever line of bullshit he was about to throw out? Go with it. It was obvious to me that he was the master and I was the wingman.

One night after I finished busking, I returned to *The Dubliner* to have a beer and catch the end of his show. The band was on a break and Skirm was talking to a man at a table across the room. He saw me order my beer and called me over. He politely introduced me to a drunken Norwegian and they continued chatting and toasting glasses. After about the second pint, me still on my first, Skirm looked at me and raised his eyebrows. Okay, here we go. I don't know where this is going? But I am along for the ride.

Skirm challenged the Norwegian guy to a beer chugging contest. They counted to three, tapped pints on the table and began to chug. Skirm let the Norwegian win and I knew it. I had seen Skirm chug beers before and obviously he threw that competition. Then he challenged the guy to a rematch. The Norwegian agreed and ordered two more pints. Skirm just looked at me and smiled as I sipped my beer. Two more beers arrived and once again they repeated the contest and again Skirm let the Norwegian win. Skirm slammed his pint glass on the table and said, "Damn, you beat me again, and I was the champion."

He congratulated the blushing drunken man and slapped him on the back. Then Skirm said:

"I may have been the champ before, but do you know who the champ is now?" The Norwegian looked confused as Skirm pointed at me. The Norwegian looked at my skinny, American frame in disbelief. Skirm knew I couldn't chug a beer to save my life. He said he wanted a rematch against me to reclaim his title. I just said *No.* Skirm raised his eyebrows and just kept challenging me. "I am going to kick your ass. You may be the champ now, but I got you this time." I had no idea where this was going? Skirm just looked at me and smiled with the devil's look in his eyes. There is no way I can beat him.

Skirm continued to taunt me with my standard reply of *No, this is not happening*. Two more beers arrived at the table, Skirm continued to challenge me, when the Norwegian threw two hundred Kroner (about 20 euros) on the table and said to me, "I think he can beat you."

Once again, Skirm looked at me, and again I said *No*. He insisted with, "Come on, you Yankee Cunt." I said *No* again and the guy threw another two hundred on the table. Skirm smiled and I said *No* again but he continued to challenge me. Once again I said *No* and the Norwegian guy kept throwing money on the table. When the money got high enough, Skirm raised his eyebrows again. I said, *Fine, I don't want to embarrass you in front of your friend, but there's no way you're going to beat me*. We counted to three, tapped our glasses on the table and I slowly sipped my beer while Skirm swallowed his like a vacuum. He slammed his glass down on the table and let out a big yell explaining he was the champion again. I congratulated him on his victory and regaining his title. I told them I guess I had lost my edge, as Skirm grabbed the cash and stuck it in his pocket. Not long after, I finished my beer and left the bar to go to the flat I shared upstairs with Skirm and the band. The band finished their last set of the show, and about forty five minutes later, Skirm walked through the flat door laughing. With a beer in his hand, he strolled over to me confidently and said, "Here's your half" and handed me a wad of cash. We both busted out laughing and toasted with a beer. We pulled that hustle several more times over the next week. It worked like a charm. When the money got high enough I took the bet and we split the cash. Not only did we take the money, but somehow Skirm had convinced the others to buy all the beers as well. It was classic.

Maybe I should have felt bad about running the scam. But I didn't. If they were dumb and drunk enough to bet their money, I was going to take it. I was making more money off beer chugging contests then I was busking on the street and I got free beer as well. I never played *Johan Gate* again.

Welcome To The Dark Side

It was a warm summer afternoon in Oslo, Norway and I had the night off. I spent the afternoon at a local beach when I returned to *The Dubliner* downstairs from my flat for a beer. While most Norwegians were outside enjoying the summer weather, I sat with a few others at the bar in the shade sucking up the air from the fans. Through a random meeting, I began a conversation with a Norwegian woman sitting at the bar. She was a few years older than me, well-dressed, wearing a cute denim mini skirt with tights and a blouse. She had beautiful brown eyes and dark hair which was different from a lot of the other typical blonde Norwegians I was used to seeing. She noticed the tattoo on my arm and asked me about it. We began to chat and I told her I was a musician and she told me that she was an artist as well. She did sketches and paintings, but her favorite thing to do was sculpture. She had done a lot in the past and recently had a big art show in Oslo. Intrigued by the artistic connection, we continued to talk and decided to head down to the harbor for another drink and watch the sunset. On an old wooden boat that had been converted into a bar, the drinks continued to flow along like a scene in a movie. We had another drink by candlelight before we exited the boat and I walked her to the water taxi stand nearby. Things were going well on this chance encounter, but I was still not sure if she was interested in me or not? When we arrived at the dock, we realized she had missed the last ferry to her home in the country outside of Oslo. She turned to me and said, "I guess I will have to take a taxi. Do you want to come with me and see the countryside?" *Yahtzee*! I am in.

We walked the short way to a normal taxi stand and she grabbed my hand as we climbed in. We sat in the back and I noticed the driver was from the Middle East somewhere. At this point, it was the summer after 9/11 and tensions were high around the world. I had already taken a lot of questions about being *American,* and the situation going on with the Middle East and my country's politics. War seemed imminent at some point. I got some support from strangers, but also got a lot of negative karma aimed at me because of my nationality. It was a very sensitive time to be touring abroad. I never talk about politics, religion or money. I still don't. Many times I have walked away from a conversation if someone was too persistent or overbearing.

In the back of my mind I was nervous about the driver. He drove like a maniac and never said a word. If he asked where I was from, I was ready to answer *Canada - A,* which I have done before just to avoid any conversations or conflict. A few minutes after we left the city lights, we were flying through the Deep Norwegian Woods on a skinny two-lane road, with thick trees on each side, up and down hills, around sharp curves with no street lights. It was pitch dark with only the headlights of the taxi peering through what seemed like the back roads of West Virginia to me. We sat quietly talking in the backseat when all of a sudden the cab driver slammed on his brakes and began to scream at the top of his lungs, "*Eli…. Eli…. Eli… Eli…!!!*" I froze! He sounded like he was doing a *Muslim death call to Allah.* I thought, *Shit, he has figured out I'm American and he's going to kill me right here in the woods and leave me as a sacrifice to Allah.* I would just disappear and nobody would ever find me. I adjusted the best I could to a defense position in my seat belt in case he came over the front seat at me. I looked up and peered through the windshield. I saw what appeared to me at that time to be a dinosaur. It was huge and hairy. It towered over the taxi. It filled up the whole windshield and was looking straight at us with its eyes glowing and massive horns. What the fuck? Is that a *Norwegian Bigfoot?* The taxi driver kept yelling and blowing the horn as we watched it slowly walk off the edge of the road and step back into the dark woods. In shock, with my adrenaline pumping, I asked the driver, *What the hell was that?* He still repeated "*Eli… Eli…. Eli…!!!*" The girl beside me said "moose." Unbeknownst to me, *Eli* meant "moose" in Norwegian. I thought I was worried about being sacrificed to Allah. That was the first time I'd ever seen a moose in person. They are gigantic, bigger than a horse, and the males with their large horns can be extremely mean. If we had hit that moose, we would have knocked his skinny legs right out from underneath him. His full body, horns and all, would have come crashing straight through the windshield. That was close. I sunk back in my seat, still shaken, when the Norwegian girl grabbed my hand and we continued the journey to her country house.

She lived at the top of a hill, overlooking a Norwegian Fjord below. With the stars out and the moon shining, we sat on the front porch of her quaint little wooden home. She explained to me she loved to sleep outside. She enjoyed the fresh air and the sounds of nature. She went inside and got two thin mats, pillows and a bottle of wine. She laid the mats down on the front porch under the roof and we stretched out. We were talking, laughing and sharing drinks directly from the bottle. As time went on she went inside and came back wearing nothing but a long sleeve, white, men's dress shirt with only a few buttons fastened. She looked sexy in the moonlight and it was a signal to me that it was *Game Time.* Right here, right now, in the open air of the Norwegian countryside on her front porch.

As she got closer, in the glow of the moonlight I noticed something. She had long dark hair on her legs and a lot of it. I had not seen it before because she had been wearing tights. That's when it dawned on me that she was *a naturalist.* She was a "hippie chick" who did not believe in shaving. As her shirt dropped to the floor so did my excitement. I witnessed hair under her arms and pubic hair region that looked like an afro from an episode of *Soul Train.* I may have thought I saw *Bigfoot* earlier, now I was face-to-face with another monster in the Norwegian countryside. I believe in everyone's own personal right and choice when it comes to grooming, but I can't deal with hairy chicks. It was a deal-breaker for me. We kissed a little bit, but nothing else happened before we drifted off to sleep. I just couldn't bring myself to do it.

I slept like shit that night on that hard wooden porch. I kept thinking she had such a pretty face and a great body, what a waste that she looked like a *Chia Pet.*

In the morning when the sun came up she asked me if I wanted to come in for coffee and see some of her art. I politely said *Yes,* even though I could not wait to get out of there. Still in the nude, her hair was even more prominent now in the morning light. She walked to the coffee pot on the counter and I noticed, sitting in the middle of her round kitchen table was a bust of a man's head. It was the latest sculpture she had just finished. Half of the man's face was missing. His right eye hung out of the socket and dropped down the cheek. The bust was someone who looked like they were just shot in the face or mauled by a bear. It was gross and disturbing. I continued to look around the room at her other pictures and works of art. They were all equally horrific in nature. Paintings of people who have been cut open, body parts severed, guts exposed and blood. There was a sculpture of just a hand on her counter with a butcher knife sticking through it. It was a knife holder. This shit was dark. She was definitely from the Dark Side of Art. I felt like I was in a house of horrors and I could not wait to get out of there.

When she said she was an artist, I thought she meant landscapes and flowers. Not severed body parts and mutilation. She explained she liked this kind of art and was fascinated with the human body. The "realness" of her art is what got her into the recent art show. I politely said they were very nice while I sipped my coffee. I was wondering if she was about to kill me and make me her next model. Would she then bury me under the house like *John Wayne Gacy*?

After what I determined to be an *ample amount of time,* I told her I needed to go. I didn't have enough money for the cab fare, but I did have enough for the one-hour water taxi ride back to the harbor. She drove me in her old beat-up, *hippie car* to the dock and when the water taxi arrived we bid farewell. I never saw her again. On that beautiful ride back to Oslo harbor, I couldn't help but think about the bizarre night I had just been through. What seemed to be a sure thing, the Middle Eastern taxi driver, the moose, and the girl that turned out to be *Captain Caveman* with serial killer tendencies. I was happy to be alive and even happier still to see my own bed in the flat. That was a close one!

For reference, if you ever get a chance to travel through Norway by water, by all means do it. It is breathtakingly beautiful. As you weave in and out of those fjords, take it all in, enjoy the scenery and the traditions of Norwegian people. Just be wary of *Eli* and *Captain Caveman.*

Self-Surgery

It's been said, "Necessity is the mother of invention." Maybe so? However, when it comes to self-surgery, I do not recommend it.

In November of 2001, I was playing a month-long gig, thirty nights in a row in the posh town of St. Moritz, Switzerland. High in the southern Swiss Alps, it was breathtakingly beautiful. Now when I say posh, I mean it! It was like a little Swiss Beverly Hills, a small town where *The Rich* would go to vacation and ski. There were Rolls Royces, ankle-length fur coats and lots of champagne. You could just smell the money, and I felt completely out of place when it came to the clientele, but I was there to work. Prince Charles actually goes there to play polo on the frozen lake.

I was alone and didn't really know anyone in that town other than the people I worked with and they were just acquaintances at best. I lived alone in a flat at the bottom of *The Big Hill*. (Everywhere in Switzerland is uphill.) I spent most of my time reading books and watching *The Simpsons* dubbed in Italian. It was the last gig on my five-month tour in Europe and I was looking forward to flying home to the States for Christmas. About a week into the gig I began to notice a pain at the top of my ass crack. I thought maybe I had bumped my tailbone. I had fallen on the ice several times and figured my tailbone was just sore. After a few days I would be just fine, or so I thought.

The next few weeks went by; the pain seemed to get stronger and worse. The "sore area" was severely irritated by the seam on the back of my jeans. It hurt to sit down, stand up, and bend over. It got so bad that I could no longer sleep on my back. Finally, I could feel with my finger what seemed to be a pimple at the top of my ass crack. I couldn't see it because of where it was located, but I tried to pop it and nothing happened. I just went through the pain. I was about a week from my long travel home and the thought of sitting on an airplane for hours with this pain was just not possible. Like I said, I didn't know anyone in town. The option of me finding a stranger and saying, *Hey can you help me for a second?* Walk into the bathroom, dropping my pants and bending over so they can look at my ass was just not going to happen. I didn't even know if this town had a doctor. It was very remote and I didn't speak the language either. I was broke and seeing a doctor was just out of the question. I did not have the money for a hospital bill; I barely had enough money to eat.

Finally a few days before I was set to leave, I couldn't take it anymore. About 3 a.m. after my gig, I headed back to my small flat and prepared to deal with this zit myself. Armed with a needle from a hotel sewing kit, a Swiss Army knife, a shaving mirror and a bottle of Jack Daniels, I proceeded to face the problem head-on. I stripped naked, jumped onto the dresser, bent over and held out the shaving mirror to see what this thing looked like. It appeared to be a zit, about the size of a dime and had a little white head in the middle. I took a big gulp of Jack and grabbed the needle to open it up. Have you ever tried to do anything in a mirror? Everything is backward, but now I am dealing with two mirrors. One mirror behind me and one in my hand and I'm drinking. It was confusing. With a needle in one hand and still a little wobbly from the Jack, I did my best to hit the white spot head on. Pfffft! It popped! A little white substance and blood, it opened. I remember thinking, *That's it?* This was the most painful zit I have ever had in my life, and that was it? Just a little blood. Wow, that was a disappointment.

The pressure and pain were still there, but now the zit was open. I took another big gulp of Jack, grabbed my Swiss Army knife and proceeded to try and open it a little more to see if there was anything left in there to come out. I put the blade into my ass crack on top of the zit and pulled slightly upward. What happened next was nothing short of a horror movie.

The top of my ass crack exploded like a grenade. A mixture of blood and a green, yellow, gray and white substance exploded across the mirror and the wall beside it in a horizontal direction about six feet across. I had some sort of fluid running out of my ass crack like a faucet and I freaked out. The mirror and the wall looked like I had just shot someone in the head. The smell of this fluid was the most disgusting thing I had ever smelled and it was running out of me unstoppably. All I could think to do was jump in the shower. I was truly freaked out. I had no idea what was going on. What was inside of me? At the moment I began to wonder if I had been abducted by aliens while I was there.

With the shower water running over me and the fluid still running out of me, I leaned against the shower wall with one hand and put my other hand on my back to keep myself from passing out. My back exploded again. This thing that is inside of me is halfway up my back. I stroked my back downward and the fluid just kept coming. I had no idea what to do and no one to call. I was alone and had something inside of me. After about twenty minutes in the shower the fluid appeared to stop and I exited the bathroom to face the mess in the other room. There was a trail of fluid on the floor from where I ran to the shower. Stuff all over the wall and the smell was making me gag. I opened the windows even though it was about minus ten degrees Fahrenheit and tried to air out my room. I shivered in the cold as I was trying to clean up the massacre, occasionally running back to the shower to relieve more of this fluid. It was a nightmare and I still had no idea what this was. And I was alone.

For the next several days and nights, I got in the shower several times a day and drained whatever was inside of me. It was gross and disgusting, but at least the pressure and pain had gone down. I walked around for days with toilet paper between my ass cheeks in case it opened again and started to drain. It was not pretty. I remember playing one night when I leaned over to change a foot pedal and I felt it open up. I took a break and went to the bathroom. It drained again, not only did I have to change the toilet paper, but I threw my underwear away. It was a horrible week. I never went for medical treatment and didn't tell anyone until my last night of the gig. The horrible part was over, the draining had stopped for the most part, and I was headed home for Christmas. On the last evening I had dinner with two musician friends of mine who were taking over for me during the month of December. They were a married couple from Hawaii and they had a good laugh when I told them about my horrifying ordeal. Strangely enough, when I returned in January, I found out the female had the same thing happen to her during the month of December and spent four days in the hospital to have it removed. I personally know two other musicians who have had the same thing happen to them during THAT gig. We all have no idea why. Maybe it has something to do with the altitude? Or just bad luck? The three of us all had it and it's painful and not fun.

I never sought medical treatment and I still have a scar at the top of my ass crack from the Swiss Army knife and I have a flare up from time to time. It just drains a little and then goes away. It was still uncomfortable, but not nearly as bad as it was a few months ago. I have dealt with this thing for fourteen years. A few months ago I had another flare-up and finally went to the doctor. He diagnosed me immediately. It turns out I had a *Pilonidal Cyst* and I need to have surgery. All these years later, I had it taken care of by a medical professional and hopefully will not have any more trouble.

Like I said before, *Necessity is the mother of invention,* unless it comes to self-surgery. I don't recommend it, see a professional.

Holly Jolly Christmas

In December of 2001 I had just finished a three-month tour of Europe and I was headed home for Christmas. Months earlier I had booked my overseas flights through Amsterdam and I allowed myself four extra days off after the gig before I returned home for some R&R.

I was leaving Switzerland and I would return again in January for the ski season. On my last night one of the cooks in the kitchen approached me outside and gave me an early Christmas gift. He handed me a big bag of marijuana and said, "This is for you, safe travels and Merry Christmas." He had grown this stuff at his house and gave this big, full, bulging bag to me. Seriously, on the last day I was there? Where the hell was he at the beginning of the month when I got there? I knew I was traveling on a midnight train out of Switzerland to Germany and then to Holland. I was going through multiple countries, multiple border patrols and I was near the end of my three-month travel visa. I already look suspicious with my guitar case and there was no way I was going to take a big bag of weed with me. I smoked a joint out of it and left it for the next musicians to arrive. I never saw that bag again.

I took a slow-moving mountain train down through the Alps and proceeded on my journey to Amsterdam. I had heard stories my whole life about the coffee shops and the Red Light District, but I had never been there. I was going, I was single, traveling alone, and had a full pocket of cash from the gig. I was going to see what Amsterdam was all about.

On the train from Switzerland to Holland, I thanked God I did not take that bag of pot. I was stopped and searched five times that night by Customs Police on the trains. It seemed like every time I finally dozed off to sleep I was awakened by an armed officer shouting at me, "Papers!" I showed them all the requested paperwork, I let them and the drug dogs search me and my bags, but I was clean. I didn't get much sleep that night, but in the morning I remember looking out of the window at the Dutch landscape. It was the most fertile, green land I have ever seen, it almost glowed like neon, basking in the morning sunlight with dew on the fields. The fields disappeared and the city came to life as we pulled into Amsterdam Central Station.

It was 6 a.m. on Sunday morning, most of the town was still passed out from Saturday night, and just a few people were stumbling home or walking their dogs. I quickly carried my guitar, suitcase and backpack to the taxi stand and took off for my hotel. I booked a room for myself with a bathtub. I have not seen a bathtub in three months and I was looking forward to a long, hot, bubbly soak. I threw my belongings into the trunk of the cab, handed the driver the hotel address and we sped off through the city streets with me looking out the windows in the back trying to take in scenes of a new city. We arrived and the taxi driver grabbed my belongings and slammed the trunk shut. I paid him, he jumped back in his car, muttered something about Americans and drove away. I looked down at my bags and realized one of my *Doc Marten* dress shoes I had tied to my backpack was gone. They had come untied in the cab and one was still in the trunk of the taxi. I would never see it again. I was off to a good start, I had been in town for almost an hour, not had a drink or a smoke and I had already lost a shoe. I would normally not have been that upset, but *Doc Marten* shoes are expensive and I wore them on stage. Now I was going to have to buy a new pair.

I entered the lobby and checked in. They had my reservation, but I could not check in until after 3 p.m. They would hold my bags for me, but I was on my own until the room was ready. They called another taxi for me and I headed for the center of Amsterdam alone.

I arrived at *Dam Square* about 8 am. I paid the driver, entered into the vast Central Square and took in the 360 degree view. There were a few people milling around and I was taking pictures when I noticed a big mural of Bob Marley smoking a joint, painted on the side of a building with a sign that said *Paradise Coffee Shop*.

I made a direct line to the shop and entered into the smoky haze. The coffee shop was dimly lit, and dark. A fog of smoke-clouded, red-painted walls and reggae music played as I made my way to the counter. A gentleman walked up to me and handed me menus. He looked at me and said, "American?" I replied, *Yes*. He never said a word after that, just spun around and pulled a freshly washed marijuana pipe off the shelf behind him and handed it to me. Obviously he knows we Americans smoke it pure out of a pipe and we're not good at rolling joints.

I glanced down at the menus; one was a normal Coffee Menu with standards, espressos, mochas and more. The other was a menu for pot and hash. They also had a display case on the counter filled with pot cookies and brownies. I skimmed through the menus, ordered an Americana coffee with milk and proceeded to read the names of the pot choices. I recognized the flavors from my time at Christiania: *White Widow, Purple Haze, Jimi Hendrix* and more, when I decided to try the *Blueberry*. I like blueberries and I like pot and it was a win-win for me. He gave me a small bag. I sat down at the table with my coffee, my pipe and my bag of blueberry goodness and smoked away. There were not many people in the coffee shop about 8:30 a.m. when I started to chat with a young English gentleman sitting alone at the table next to me. Over coffee and puffs he told me that he was from London, but had been living in Amsterdam for years. I told him I was American and I was just passing through on my way home to the States and was playing tourist. I asked him what sites I should see while I was in town? He replied, "Well, you did good on your first outing." He mentioned *The Red Light District*, a few other places and *Anne Frank's House*. I knew the story of Anne Frank and I figured I might as well go and see it while I was there and get another lesson in history. He mentioned that the house was not far away. I finished my coffee and planned to head that way before the crowds got big. I bid him thank you and farewell as I attempted to stand up and exit. That's when I realized I could NOT stand up. *The Blueberry* had set in and my legs were like rubber. I ordered another cup of coffee and we laughed. We chatted a little more until I could get my composure and could actually walk out of the building.

I exited the coffee shop and knew that I was too fucked up to go to *Anne Frank's House*, and besides the English guy had warned me that the tour was deep, dark and depressing. I was high and happy, I didn't need a buzz kill. I asked a man for directions to *The Red Light District*. He pointed and I stumbled down the cobblestone streets for my first look at the world-renowned section.

When I entered the district there was not much action. *The Red Light District* is not busy on a Sunday morning, the day of God. Most of the windows had curtains drawn over them with signs that said closed. Only a few girls danced in the windows and they were not the attractive kind to me. Most everything was closed with just a few people passing on the streets when I entered a mini mart to buy a Coke and some postcards. I made my purchase and continued down the street when a Street Barker motioned me to come into a place that was open. At this point I had been up all night and was stoned and exhausted. I didn't really care if I had a beer or a Coke, all I knew was I just wanted a bath and a nap in my hotel room. When I entered the bar I had no idea it was a strip club. Of course, I should have maybe figured that out, but my senses were not at their best and I obviously looked like an out-of-place American Tourist, whether I liked it or not. I didn't care.

There were a handful of men in there, but mostly empty tables and chairs. I sat down at the bar, ordered a Heineken and paid no attention to the empty stage across the room when I began to write my postcards home. I heard Lenny Kravitz's version of *American Woman* come to life through the sound system and briefly glanced up at the stage to see a young lady walk on wearing an American flag bikini. I thought to myself, *Nice touch---American Woman, American flag bikini, she was smart enough to work it.* I turned my attention back to writing my postcards.

A few seconds later, I felt a hand on my right elbow and looked up from my writing. It was the girl from the stage with her Star-Spangled Glory. She pulled me away from my postcards and led me on stage.

She motioned for me to sit down in a chair in the middle of the stage. Having respect for her showmanship as a performer and her choice of music and costume, I played along. I sat down, she took off my shirt and pulled out a set of handcuffs. She cuffed my hands behind the chair then blindfolded me. Okay, I was a little uneasy about this; was I about to be robbed or beaten? Or both? I kept my composure as the men in the audience began to yell and cheer. All I know is she was doing something on stage, but she was not touching me in any way, and I couldn't see a thing.

In a flash she stood me up and laid me flat on my back in the middle of the stage, still handcuffed and blindfolded. The men continued to hoot and holler as she removed the blindfold from my face. She was squatted over me with her shaved, bare pussy about three inches from my face. She was grinding in front of me, and I couldn't move. She looked down at me and said something I will never forget, "Okay American boy, I bet you have never seen anything like this before." She produced a vibrator from behind her back and began to fuck herself right there in front of my face close up. I replied, *Oh contraire, but I have seen that before.* She kept grinding when she reached down to the end of the toy and popped off the cap and exposed a magic marker. She placed the marker on my chest, with the little toy still inside her and began to draw. The men yelled, and I had no idea what she was doing. Playing Tic-Tac-Toe? I didn't care, it was all part of the show. As the song ended with a single beat, she pulled me to my feet and spun me around to face the audience. On my chest with magic marker she had written "The End." She quickly uncuffed me, grabbed her clothes and blew me a kiss as she exited the stage. I never saw her again. Now five minutes later I am back at the bar writing my postcards. I finished my beer and walked out of the bar still amazed with what just happened. It was now almost 10 a.m. and I've only been in town for a few hours and now I'm walking through *The Red Light District*, still stoned and buzzed from a beer and I have "The End" written on my chest in magic marker from a stripper. This was going to be an interesting few days as I made my way back to a taxi stand and headed to the hotel again.

The International Bobsled Team

In hindsight, it may have been one of the dumbest, unsafe things I have ever done in my life, but certainly one of the most fun.

In January of 2002 I took a month-long gig back in St. Moritz, Switzerland, for the ski season. I was playing at a posh hotel every night for a month. When I arrived at the train station, I recognized a guy I had seen a few months before when I was playing there in November. I remembered him because he was one of the most striking, handsome men I have ever seen. Being a straight male, I was even surprised by my own observation, but he was young, well-built and strappingly handsome. He worked loading and unloading the trains as they arrived at the station. He looked like he should have been on magazine covers. The women who saw him just gushed over him.

A few nights into my gig, I saw him arrive at the pub where I was playing and I said *hello*. His name was Ramon, he was from Milan, Italy and spoke no English. Through our awkward language barrier, we became friends and spent the whole month together hanging out. St. Moritz is a very small town and to meet a local was kind of nice. We could go to dinner and hang out at the other bars after the show and flirt with girls. He was a nice, fun guy and we had a lot of laughs even though we could not talk to each other. We had a very "caveman-like" relationship. Lots of pointing, grunts, smiles and laughs. I would love to see him again.

I learned a lot of things from Ramon. One was how to take the tobacco out of a cigarette and replace it with pot without tearing the paper. He also showed me how to remove the filter and it looked like you were smoking a regular cigarette. It was genius, and long before blunts were popular.

One afternoon we found an English/Italian dictionary. We learned a lot about each other over beers that afternoon. I learned he was the Italian National Champion for bodybuilding in his weight class. That explained his well-built physique. He was an uncle of a sweet little girl and wanted to introduce me to his sister in Milan. If she was as good-looking as he was, I was in, but it never happened. When he came into the bar at night, women just flocked around him. I used to hang out with him just for the leftovers.

Not long after my return to St. Moritz, Ramon and I were out drinking after the show one night when he introduced me to a lovely Swiss girl named Claudia. She was a local, and I had noticed her in November when I was there, but I was still too shy to speak. She was blond-haired, blue-eyed and kind of shy, but very sweet. We hit it off and began dating for the rest of the month that I was there.

During the height of that month in the winter season, St. Moritz was booming with people and winter activities. St. Moritz hosted a World Championship Downhill Ski Competition while I was there. There were curling matches where you can sip champagne and watch people slide silly little rocks down the ice. I still don't understand that game. I think it's more about drinking and being seen than anything else.

They also had a luge track and a championship bobsled competition while I was there, and she took me to see it. I have always been a fan of bobsledding since I was a kid, but I had never seen it live in person. It was awesome and breathtaking. Seeing those sleds go down that ice around one hundred miles an hour on sharp, banked curves - I was hooked. The track was a mile long and went down over one thousand feet in elevation. The finish line was in the next tiny little village below. I was obsessed with it! You could pay to take a ride on a bobsled down the track, but it was expensive and I was broke, so that was just not going to happen. Later that evening after the race, we returned to her flat for dinner before my show. She wanted to cook some real traditional Swiss food for me and we enjoyed a Swiss drink called *Flamli*. (A mixed drink containing dry vermouth and blended whiskey.) We had several. Somewhere in the evening conversation, me still fascinated with the bobsled, she mentioned that her next-door neighbor worked on the bobsled track. I immediately exited her flat and knocked on the neighbor's door. That is when I met Alex.

Alex was from England and worked on the crew that maintained the pristine track that was unachievable to me. We returned to Claudia's flat and after a few more drinks I had more questions for Alex. Our conversation went like this.

Me - *Hypothetically, is there any kind of security on the bobsled run?*

Alex - "No."

Me - *No cameras or anything?*

Alex - "Only the TV cameras when they are racing."

Me - *I wonder how far someone would get if they rode something down that run?*

Alex - "You mean like a bobsled?"

Me - *No, like a hotel tray?*

Alex - "I don't know, but I would like to find out?"

Me - *Meet me at 2 a.m. after my show.*

After the show Ramon and I swiped a few hotel trays from the kitchen and headed out. We met up with Claudia, Alex and three Army friends of mine that came to visit me from their base in Ramstein, Germany. We trudged up the snow- and- ice-covered hill until we reached the starting gate. We aligned our trays end to end, wrapped our arms and legs around each other and pushed off down the hill. At this point, I need to mention that professional bobsled riders wear helmets, goggles, knee and elbow pads and safety suits. They also have medical teams on standby, and most importantly a highly engineered bobsled. We were drunk, wearing no pads and on hotel trays.

The ride started off slow and picked up speed quickly. What happened next was an experience of giant white walls of ice, flashes of the dark sky whizzing by left and right, treetops, screams and bouncing off ice walls all lit up by the blue Swiss full moonlight. Every once in a while I would get a quick glimpse of the moon, but it disappeared quickly out of view over the sides of the wall. We arrived at the final horseshoe turn and rocketed into the soft snow at the finish line. It was over as quickly as it started and we all had a look of shock, horror and amazement amongst thunderous laughter of what we had just done. We had totally underestimated the speed at which we would be traveling and the thrill of the ride. We all sat in the snowbank as Alex rolled a joint on the back of his tray. We laughed and talked about what just happened then realized we had a problem. We were in the next village a mile away downhill and no way to get back to St. Moritz without walking uphill. It was the middle of the night and the buses didn't run anymore. Alex decided to call a taxi and the driver picked us up at the bottom and took us back to the top for another ride.

We rode another one or two times that night before returning to our homes. Each time we got to the bottom, Alex called the cab again. We decided to call ourselves *The International Bobsled Team*, because we were all from different countries. We had four Americans, one Swiss, one Italian and one Brit.

In the morning, my friends and I were laughing and recalling the previous night's events. We compared matching bruises on all of our knees and elbows from smashing against the ice walls at high speed. We were bruised and sore, but didn't care and we did it again the next night.

Over the next few weeks we shared our little bobsled secret with a few select people. We are told some English soldiers on vacation about our excursions, and they joined us on more than one occasion. They liked to stealthily sneak down the track a few hundred yards and jump on the track after we went by, chasing us like an ambush. Yelling and screaming, they would come from behind you like you were being chased by a *Swiss Yeti*. We knew it was them and they were a bunch of nuts. One night one of the English soldiers had his sport coat completely ripped in half on a run. As the popularity of our late-night hijinks grew, so did the amount of people doing it. Hotels and bars were beginning to wonder why their trays were disappearing. We had them hidden all over town, under trash cans, behind walls and bushes. We all had our own personal tray, and suspicion was beginning to arise as the month came to a close. I rode that bobsled run more times and I can remember. On my last run, I decided to go down the run alone. No one had the balls to do it at this point; we all went in groups like a toboggan. I took on the challenge.

My friends went first and I gave out a yell from the top of the hill when they were to start the timer. I took a running start and hopped on for the final ride.

Normal bobsled teams make the mile long run in a time of about 1:02, doing approximately one hundred miles per hour. My time was 2:04. I was doing approximately fifty miles an hour on a hotel tray alone. We learned early on to hold on tight to the tray, because if you lost it, you were still going down the track only this time on your ass.

As the month drew to an end I prepared to travel on my tours. We all signed my tray and I mailed it home to the States. I still have it. It's cracked, scratched and missing a corner but it is still a great memory of some wild times in the Swiss Alps.

Once again, it was one of the dumbest things I have ever done from a safety standpoint, but also one of the most fun. I would do it again in a heartbeat, but this time I would wear pads and a helmet.

The Jumper And The Creeper

People are strange. Over my many years of being on stage and on this planet, I've met a lot of people. Everyone is different and has their own personality and quirks. From their personal fashion style, what they drink, to their interest and hobbies. I *NEVER* seem to be amazed or surprised. There are some sick people out there and I have seen more than my share. There is always something out there that makes me go *huh?*

One of those strange memories occurred in the winter of 2002 when I was playing in St. Moritz, Switzerland.

The *Stubli Pub* where I played was dark, smoky, hot and small. It was in the basement of one of the biggest, most expensive hotels in town, *The Schweizerhof Hotel*. The downstairs where I played looked more like a dungeon. When I say small, I mean it. It was one of the smallest rooms I have ever played. It probably was about forty feet long and thirty feet across with a tiny four foot by four foot stage tucked in the corner. The opposite corner from the stage was a wooden bar about twenty five feet long. The walls were dark wood, stained with the years of smoke and spilled beer. The wall to the right of the stage was old stone, also smoke stained, with stained glass windows. Very medieval looking. The wooden floor was filled with aged picnic tables adorned with candles and benches on each side. The windows did not open, and at night the crowd and the heat of the candles made it hot. Minus zero degrees Fahrenheit outside; inside over one hundred degrees in that pub. It was small and always cramped at night. Asshole to belly button, with people everywhere, it was almost impossible to move through the room.

They crammed over one hundred people in that room like sardines. Apparently, Switzerland did not have a fire occupancy code, or at least they were not following it. God forbid if a fire had broken out, we all would have died running to the one and only exit near the stage.

I still don't know how waiters made it through the crowd. I would see just an arm sticking up through the crowd holding a full tray of *Warsteiner* beer. Every once in a while someone would bump the waiter and the whole tray would just crash down raining beer and glass on the people below. The waiter would just fill another tray and try it again.

It was packed and hard to move in that room every night. I actually had trouble getting off the stage to go outside for a cigarette on my break. It would take me a few minutes to squeeze through the crowd to get to the door even though I was only about fifteen feet away. Getting back on the stage after the break was also equally challenging. People spilled out the door into the long hallway just trying to get inside.

Already in the peak of the ski season, the tiny Swiss town was busy both day and night. People were on the slopes in the daytime and at night in the bars and restaurants. After the slopes were closed there was nothing else to do but drink. The crowd was mostly International and all letting go for a wild vacation getaway. A large group of about twenty British men was infused among the mix.

The British men were the *Queen's Footmen* on a month-long annual holiday. Every year these soldiers who stood silently day after day at attention among the crowds of tourists and picture-takers in England were ready to let off some steam. The *Queen's Footmen* are the ones you always see in the photos, standing outside Buckingham Palace in their red jackets with big fluffy black hats at full attention. No expression on their faces and in full British tradition. They stand silent on guard for eleven months out of the year, and when they get their month-long break they are ready to take full advantage of it. They terrorize that little Swiss town for one month every year. Having spent most of their time in silent attention, when it came time for a break they have a lot to make up for. They were loud, rowdy and pretty much drunk most of the time. They were all nice and respectful to me.

As an American, I usually bond pretty well with the British and they were no different. Both equally proud of our countries, we bonded over a common language and our alliance in the world. I never liked to be *The Loud American*, unless I have to. I always try to speak softly and keep my presence *under the radar* so to speak. Some other not so well-traveled Americans do not fare so well.

One night on stage, with a packed room, the *guards* were drinking in the bar per usual. Occasionally, they all would toast and I would say the phrase, *To the Queen*. The *footmen* loudly shouted the same response and then drank. No harm done, just part of the show and acknowledgement of our allies.

That night I said my British toast phrase and heard a little voice to my left in a clear American accent say, "Fuck the queen." In horror, I glanced to see a small, young, skinny-looking backpacker guy leaning up against the wall next to the stage. He was obviously American by his accent and apparently not well traveled. I looked at him like, *You stupid son of a bitch*, and then turned away guarding my guitar next to my belly to protect it from what I knew what was about to happen. I heard the crash and a brief scream as about seven *guards* rushed the guy and pinned him against the wall like a rugby team. He was pressed against the wall like a cat that had been flattened by a steamroller. One guy had him by the throat as he tried to squirm and kick back among the fury of punches that were being thrown. I guess he learned his lesson. I bet he never said that phrase again. He disappeared right after that and I never saw him again. The *guards* went back to drinking.

Movement in the *Stubli* was so hard that one of the *guards* decided it was easier to jump from table to table rather than cross the floor. I nicknamed him *The Jumper*.

I watched him night after night jump from table to table, to the bar, then back again to another table filled with drinks and candles. Most of the time drinks would be spilled and booze and glass would go flying among the laughter. He found this to be a more fun way of moving through the crowd, and executed it like an aerial chess match. None of the bar's staff ever said anything to him because they were spending so much money in the bar. After a few times of watching his drunken gymnastics, I learned that occasionally he would miss. He would misjudge the distance of the table and just land in the crowd like an awkward stage dive. I would usually hear a loud crash if I hadn't seen it, followed by two feet sticking up among the heads of the patrons. It got to the point that I would watch him and hope he missed just so I could see it happen. It helped pass the time.

The *Jumper* also had a friend who had an equally strange hobby. They called him *The Creeper*. He was like a bad Spider-Man without the costume. This particular *guard* liked to inch his way around the room holding onto the wooden trimming that lined the top of the walls. Inch by inch he would slowly creep his way around the room holding on to the thin wooden path by only his fingertips. His feet hung below him as he encircled the barroom. It was weird, like a big cockroach. I would watch him night after night along with *The Jumper*. He would make his way behind the bar, down the wall, past the door until eventually making his way over to the stage. I would step forward on the tiny stage and let him pass behind me and keep going. He would repeat the same pattern all night. It was a weird hobby, but he seemed harmless and he must have had very strong fingertips.

I spent a month with those crazy *guards*, *The Jumper* and *The Creeper* in tow. They even joined us later on late night excursions to the bobsled track. They were a lot of fun to watch and I hope they still go there and terrorize that tiny Swiss town every year.

Nowadays every time I see a picture of *The Queen's Footman*, I wonder if it's *The Jumper* or *The Creeper*?

Playing On The Titanic

I have worked for years on cruise ships and I live on an island. Strangely enough I have diagnosed myself to the best of my ability of having a form of *Aquaphobia,* a persistent and abnormal fear of water.

I do not like large bodies of water that I cannot see the bottom of or what lies beneath the surface. It freaks me out, especially at night. Maybe I have this fear from seeing *Jaws* as a young kid or swimming in local lakes of Pennsylvania that I know were man-made. Dams were built all over the country, flooding low-lying valleys and small towns to create recreation areas without clearing the land first. They flooded trees, houses and even farms beneath those waters and as a kid I heard stories about people jumping off the rocks and getting tangled in the trees below the water and drowning. It scared me then and still does today. If I am swimming in a lake or the ocean and something brushes up against me below the surface, it freaks me out completely. Even though it may just be a fish, it might as well be the Loch Ness Monster to me. To further my fears I am extremely uncomfortable with large bodies of water at night and seeing the movie *Titanic* did not help at all. When I'm working on cruise ships I do not like to go out on the deck at night. The only time I will is to have a cigarette on a break and even then I stand very close to the doorway. I can picture the boat moving and me plummeting over the edge into the icy waters below, and that is it. Never to be seen again. I have heard stories and been on ships when someone went overboard and was never found. What a horrible way to die. Not to mention it is my experience the farther north you go on the planet the darker and murkier the waters become. I have sailed the Baltic Sea and North Sea many times and they are almost black. I have talked to scuba divers who have told me the visibility under those waters is almost zero. I prefer the crystal clear, blue waters of the Caribbean or Mediterranean. With that being said, despite my fears I continued to work many ships over the years.

I got a job offer to work one of the finest ships to sail on the North Sea. It was the newest ship from a company called Color Line. It was state-of-the-art, much better than some of the previous older ships I had played. It sailed between Oslo, Norway, and Germany. The gig was new on the circuit and the money was better than average. The agent wanted to send some of his top players to make a good impression on the company when I got the call. I had heard from other players who have done that gig that the female Cruise Manager ran a tight ship and was very strict. The staff always seemed to be on the edge of getting in trouble and being fired. They had a no second chance policy and it made the staff more uptight. I didn't care. I could handle myself. My first experience on the ship was with the lady Cruise Manager. She gave me the general rules about conduct and the gig. Nothing new. She had an arrogance of, "I am better than you and do as I say or else." She was in complete charge, far different from other cruise managers I had worked with in the past who were generally pretty cool. I let her believe what she wanted, but she couldn't do what I did and I knew it. She was throwing around her false sense of power. *Big fucking deal!* I set up in the pub and did a sound check before returning to my cabin on the sixth floor.

I returned for my gig that first night and met a young Swedish bartender named Mikey. Maybe in his mid-twenties? He was short, pudgy and had a freaky European haircut. He was working with me for two weeks and also gave me the attitude of I am in charge around here. "This is my Pub and I run it." After exchanging professional pleasantries, I began to set up my equipment. I noticed Mikey putting on a wireless headset microphone. Out of curiosity I asked him what it was for? He replied, "I'm going to sing along with you. They hired me here because I'm such a great singer. I am just going to sing along with you and the songs I know, maybe even do a few on my own." *Oh hell no! I'm not somebody's karaoke guitar player. I don't even know this guy, I have never heard him sing and now we are a duo? NOT going to happen! They hired me, not me and my karaoke wannabe.* I immediately turned to the soundboard next to the stage and pressed a few buttons I knew he would not understand and - ta dah! his headset microphone did not come through the speakers. I watched him panic as he thought it was broken. "It worked the night before and now nothing?" He explained how he had spent a lot of his own money to buy this thing and now it was broken. He was infuriated and actually sent it back to the company for repair. I heard later from another musician he got it back six weeks later with a note from the company that said it works fine. I dodged that unforeseen bullet and I didn't have to play along with his silly musical games.

For the first week I did my job and kept a low profile. I stayed clear of most of the managers and I became friends with the other musicians who were cool. There was a Bulgarian band that played on the Sundeck and in the main Showroom with the dancers. The Bulgarian piano player who had lived in Norway for many years was named Mickey. He looked like Rod Stewart. I also met a lovely jazz singer named Magdi Bodi. Magdi was about twenty years older than me, but we became close. She was like a mother figure to me. She sang in The Jazz Lounge upstairs and had a great voice. In her younger years she was a famous girl rock icon in Hungary. She had many hits and did big shows, but now she sang Jazz and did it well. She was funny, high maintenance in a way, but I enjoyed many afternoons with Magdi and Mickey for coffee in Germany or Oslo. The tension of the Cruise Manager and the staff was a common topic among our conversations.

As entertainers we were considered to be part of the crew, but we were treated like second-class citizens when it came to the staff. We ate in the crew mess with the staff, but no one hardly ever talked to us. When I bought a drink, even Coke or water while working, I had to pay for it full price. No free drinks. We were not supposed to drink in public in front of the customers or on the ship at all. If we ate in one of the restaurants on the ship there was no employee discount like the rest of the staff. We were not permitted to use the gym, steam rooms or sauna in the fitness center because we were crew and they were for customers only. We had to pay for internet access if we wanted it, but only during the time in port because at sea it was for the passengers. The access code was different every day and sometimes they would give it to me and sometimes not. We would be virtually ignored by the staff unless they had a problem and the final blow was no crew sale. On every boat I have ever worked they have what is called a *Slobbi* sale. One day a week the crew was allowed to go to the tax-free shop and buy whatever they wanted; cigarettes, booze, clothing, cologne, food, etc. at a highly discounted rate. Every crew member I have ever met looked forward to the *Slobbi* sale. The rest of the crew got it but we musicians had to pay full price for everything. So we bought our booze and cigarettes in Germany and smuggled them back on board because it was a lot cheaper than Norway.

About two weeks into the gig, it was a Friday night and the boat was packed full of passengers headed to Germany. I had a great show and the bar was rocking, people singing along and dancing. The crowd was so big that they spilled out of the bar down the central Promenade Deck. The Pub was not used to that big of a rowdy, fun crowd. The bar staff was *in the weeds*, mixing drinks as I gave that crowd all I had. It was a great show and a great night, we all made a lot of money, tips were good. The next morning I was awakened by a knock at my cabin door from the Cruise Manager. She reprimanded me for having such a loud and rowdy crowd in the Pub the night before. The front desk had received noise complaints from the passengers above about the music and the noise of the crowd. This was not the kind of entertainment they wanted. They were a "High-class ship" and wanted me to calm it down or I would be fired. That is not what I do, but with two weeks left in the month-long gig, I was already unhappy and so I would play along. I decided if quiet is what they want, quiet is what they will get. I hurt them where it hurts the most in their wallet. I played the next two nights so quietly you could barely hear me in the Pub. I sang the most dull, boring, soft slow songs I could think of in barely a whisper. I didn't chat with the customers and I would just say thank you at the end of every song. The Pub was empty and nobody made any money. The bartenders were pissed. Two days later the lady Cruise Manager approached me again and told me to continue my normal show and get people in the Pub. I had made my point, but she was not happy having to surrender to me. She finally got the point: *Never fuck with the person who has the microphone.*

I went back to doing my normal show and the crowds came back like usual, but I did not like the way things were run on the ship by the higher-ups.

After returning to my cabin one night, I climbed into my bunk, turned on the TV and drifted off to sleep. I was in my last week and I couldn't wait for the month to end. In the middle of the night I got up to go to the bathroom. I sat on the edge of my bunk and put my feet onto the floor. In the darkness I felt my bare feet drop into about an inch of ice cold water. I froze in fear! I'm on the sixth floor so there should not be any water on this deck. I immediately began hearing Celine Dion singing in my head as I leapt for my porthole window and threw back the curtains. *Holy Shit We're Goin Down!* I peered through the window expecting to see the horizon on a slant. I gazed as the sun was coming up as normal and the ship was moving along at a normal speed. No alarms had sounded and there was water all over my cabin. With my heart racing I threw a towel around me and busted out into the hallway to look for anyone else. There was no one. All alone in the hallway I stood there and tried to figure out what was going on. The carpet in the hallway was dry, but my room was quickly flooding. I returned and sat down on my bed to catch my breath. I called the reception to make them aware of this issue. They sent a maintenance man to my cabin and discovered the cold water pipe to the shower in the cabin above me had broken and caused the flood in my room. Holy shit, I was the only cabin in the whole ship that was affected. I thought I was going to die. They cleaned up the water with a vacuum and put a giant industrial fan in my room that sounded like an airplane. The next morning I told the Cruise Manager what had happened and I needed to move to another cabin. I couldn't sleep with the sound of this big fan and I needed another room until it was dry. With no other crew cabins available, she was forced to move me into a guest cabin and would lose the sale of the room. She wasn't happy, but what else was I supposed to do? She also told me she sensed I was not happy with the ship and if I wanted, she could find a replacement to come on early and finish my last three gigs on the boat.

I had already made up my mind I wasn't going to do this gig ever again anyway. She was quite surprised when I told her I had no problem with the ship, that it was beautiful and the passengers were nice. I just didn't like the extreme paranoia of the staff, always scared they were going to be fired and on constant edge for company spies. This company had hired people to board the ship as passengers to observe the staff and report back to management. Employees would be fired immediately if they did something wrong. It was very uncomfortable. I told her I would gladly work out my remaining shows like a professional and honor my contract. She asked me if I would consider working on this boat again? I replied, *No.* When she asked why, I told her, *I have worked on a lot of ships for years and I enjoy them, but I don't want to work on a ship that is run like Nazi Germany. I am an artist and I don't like the way you treat me or the staff. You're like the Gestapo. I don't want to work in a place like this.* The look on her face was priceless, one of anger and contempt. My comment went over like a piece of shit in a punch bowl. I loved it and I didn't care; besides I would never work for that bitch again.

I spent my last three nights in a guest cabin. My final show was on route from Oslo to Germany. I already had a return flight ticket from Oslo. I could have caught a flight from Germany but I didn't want to spend the extra money and lose the round trip. On my final night I met up with the next musician and gave him the scoop about the gig. Who to watch out for, who was cool and who couldn't be trusted. The next morning when we got back to Oslo, I was one of the first ones off the boat. All they saw was the bottoms of my feet and my ass that they could kiss. I never worked that boat again.

Later when I got paid for the gig, my agent informed me the last night I had spent on the boat back to Oslo, the Cruise Manager charged me full price for that cabin because I was considered a passenger and not working. They took it out of my pay. *Bitch!!!*

A few years later I was informed they had new management on that boat, The Cruise Manager had been let go. They asked me if I was interested in doing another gig on there? I said, *NO.*

You're Bleeding

In the summer of 2003 things were beginning to pick up for me and my career after 9/11 in the USA. I had been touring Europe *HARD* for three years and spent more time in Europe than I had in the USA.

After I returned from my last tour in Europe, I began to receive calls back in Nashville. I booked a six-week tour that included shows in Atlanta, Myrtle Beach, Key West and San Antonio.

I had opportunities, more now than before and I was headed out on the road again. This time instead of foreign trains and buses, I was driving my own car. Some of the gigs were pretty high-profile to me and a lot was riding on my performances.

I hit the road and did the show in Atlanta and then headed to Myrtle Beach for three nights at *Bummz Beach Club* on Ocean Drive. I had played *Bummz* before, but this time I had a booking agent coming to see me play for the first time. He had gigs all over the country and I needed to look and sound good. I had never met him before and I was already nervous about making a good impression.

My cousins that I stayed with in Myrtle Beach always had a lot of animals at their house. There were cats, dogs and the occasional bird. This time when I visited they had three dogs; a little mutt mix, a bulldog and a big white lab named Rudy that was a retired drug dog from the police department.

The two smaller dogs lived inside the house. Rudy lived in the fenced-in backyard near the screened patio. When I would go outside in the morning to have coffee on the patio, Rudy would come to the screen and just bark. I assumed he barked because I was a stranger and he wasn't familiar with me.

I just ignored him and eventually he would go away. The pattern continued every morning and I never thought anything of it.

In the afternoon that I was supposed to play in front of the new agent, I spent the day running around town doing errands and returned to my cousin's house about an hour and a half before the show. I showered and got dressed as usual. My cousins were still at work and I let the little dog out back to pee while I was getting ready. I prepared to leave for my show then I went to the outside screen door to let the little dog back in. I cracked the door enough for him to squeeze inside under my leg without room for Rudy. The little dog slipped through as Rudy poked his head forward to get inside. I have had dogs for years and out of just natural instinct, I put my foot up to block Rudy's path of entry. Rudy's Instinct as a "police dog" kicked in at the same time.

Rudy perceived my foot as an aggressive move and bit my whole left leg above the ankle HARD! My leg was in his jaws. His top fang went through the skin and all the way to my bone. I yelled, pulled back and he let go, barking wildly. *Holy shit, that just happened and it hurts so bad!* In the blink of an eye I was bitten by a drug dog! I know what you are thinking, but NO I did not have any contraband on me and was doing nothing wrong. I just tried to let the little dog in as I have done thousands of times in my life and then I got munched on by Rudy.

Blood gushed out of my leg as I ran for the bathroom. The bleeding was bad and my girlfriend said I needed to go to the hospital. I replied, *No way, I have to play the show and there is an agent coming to see me.* With Rudy still barking outside, I slapped a makeshift bandage on the wound and headed for the show. It was still bleeding when I arrived and began to play. Occasionally I would wince in pain from the bite, but I never let it show on stage.

I spotted the agent immediately. He was sitting in the front row with a video camera filming my entire show. I continued to do what I do and never drew attention to my leg, even though I could feel the blood running down into my shoe. Finally after a while the agent approached me on stage and whispered in my ear, "Hey you know you are bleeding? You have blood running down your leg into your sock." I simply and easily replied, *Yeah I know, pay no attention.* I kept going with the show. Not long after the agent left I finished the show without another word about the blood.

When I returned home I cleaned the wound and tried to patch it up on my own without going to the doctor. That eventually didn't work. It became extremely infected and the smell coming from that wound was putrid, I had to get it treated. I got shots and antibiotics, it eventually healed and I still have a little scar. It looks like I was shot with a 22 bullet without an exit wound. When people ask me what the scar is from, I tell them, *It's from an Undercover Mission I did in Europe and I got shot. I can't talk about it.* It›s a complete lie, but I›m not giving Rudy any more attention for this one.

A week later I did finally hear from the agent. He never mentioned the blood on my leg. He must have been impressed by my performance or work ethic. I never asked him. He booked me for shows after that for years.

Rudy has since passed away, but I feel no remorse. I hated that dog.

The Road to Key West.

In the spring of 2003, I got a gig booked in Key West for the very first time. I'd never been to Key West and didn't know much about it other than Jimmy Buffett. Ralph Murphy, my ASCAP rep, referred me to the manager of a bar called *The Hog's Breath Saloon*. They hired a lot of Nashville acts and due to my recommendation, Charlie Bauer, the manager, took a chance on me and booked me for the last two weeks of August for a tryout. I was excited for the new opportunity.

I was starting to grow tired from all my long tours in Europe and was looking forward to spending more time at home in my own country. I had been on the road hard for years and my last tax return showed that I had only spent four days at home in Nashville for the whole year. The rest of the time I was on the road playing.

In the late spring I received a phone call from a piano player friend of mine in New York City named Richie Campbell, about a gig in Key West. There was an ad in the local paper that said, "Solo players needed for a high-energy traffic bar in Key West." He called the number and talked to a guy named Irish Kevin. Kevin explained to him that they were only looking for guitar players, not piano players. The gig was four hours long with no break. The Entertainer must be able to sing, play, be personable, funny and able to engage the crowd and hold their attention with whatever may happen. In short, the Entertainer needed to be half Musician, half Carnival Barker, half Comedian and half Master of Ceremonies. It was a tough marathon gig. Kevin asked him if he knew anyone that he thought could handle a gig like this? Richie replied, "I know one guy," then he called me.

I called the number he gave me and spoke with Irish Kevin for the first time. Irish Kevin back then and still today is a man of few words. He is trustworthy and has a heart of gold, but he only tells you what you need to know and nothing more. He doesn't elaborate on pointless things. He explained the gig was four hours long with no break. I would play on a *tryout* basis four days a week for two weeks, he would pay for my travel and give me a hotel room. That was it. Kevin never really went into the dynamics of the bar and the crowds. I was nervous about the four-hour gig, but I knew I had enough material and as long as I picked up a few Jimmy Buffett songs, I could probably fake my way through it.

I sent Kevin my press kit and my latest CD, and a few leaks weeks later he booked me for the last two weeks of July. He would be on vacation at that time, but he would send me my plane tickets and the other managers would take care of me and help me if I needed anything. That was it. I was booked for two weeks and walked into Irish Kevin's blind.

I arrived at the Key West International Airport and was picked up by a European guy named Pavel. He just said, "You Jeff?" I said, *Yes,* and he replied, "Kevin sent me. Come with me." Kinda like a mafia thing. The next thing I know we were in his Jeep and headed downtown. I was completely lost where I was when he stopped across from *The Southern Cross Hotel* on Duval Street. He helped me get my bags out and said, "You're staying here, the bar is down the street." He got in his car and drove off. My girlfriend (later my wife) had flown to Miami and taken the bus to meet me and we checked into the hotel. It was a small room with one double bed, a toilet and a shower in the same room. No doors on the bathroom, just a curtain. We had a window air conditioner unit and a cracked Styrofoam cooler held together with duct tape for a fridge from the front desk.

It was clean and basic at least, but we were just happy to have a room. We settled in and took a brief stroll around Duval Street before returning to the hotel. When we returned, I had a voicemail from Irish Kevin saying, "I hope you made it safely. Go watch the guy on stage tonight, you are on tomorrow." That was it.

My girlfriend was tired and stayed in the room as I walked down the street to *Irish Kevin's* to check out the performer on stage. I stood across the street and peered in through the door with complete horror. Onstage was the one and only Matt "Fucking" Avery. This guy was a BEAST on stage - his presence, his voice, his guitar playing and his stage show. The crowd was going wild and screaming as he displayed an absolute Rockstar performance. I was in complete shock. I returned to the hotel and my girlfriend asked, "How was it?" I replied, *Don't unpack. I can't do what I just saw. If they want me to perform like that I am in way over my head on this one. They're going to fire my ass tomorrow and we will be on our way back to Nashville.*

The next afternoon, July 15th, 2003, I played my first show at *Irish Kevin's.* I was nervous to say the least, but I got on stage and did the best I could. The first song I ever played on that stage was *Sundown* by Gordon Lightfoot. I finished my show and much to my surprise they didn't fire me, the manager just said, "See you tomorrow."

I felt a sense of relief, but kept on my toes through the rest of my time there. I met and watched other musicians and discovered they all were different. They all have their own act and style. The most outrageous was definitely Matt Avery. Over the next week I met Jared Michael Hobgood, Dan Liguori, Yo Adrian, Gary Blodgett and Taz Shepherd. They were all very welcoming to me and helped me with anything I needed to feel comfortable. The rest of the bar staff and management was the same way. I got the feeling that they were all a big family and took care of and looked after each other. My *two-week tryout* ended and I said, *Thank you for the gig.* I flew home to Nashville never knowing if I would play at *Irish Kevin's* again.

Two weeks later I returned to Key West to play my original gig at *The Hog's Breath Saloon.* One afternoon I received a voicemail from Irish Kevin. He heard I was back in town playing *The Hog's Breath* and wanted to talk to me.

The next day I met Irish Kevin for the first time in person. He explained he wanted me to work for him at his bar. He could guarantee me at least four shows a week if I was interested in coming down to play for the winter season. I liked playing *The Hog's Breath,* but that gig was only two weeks every few months. Kevin offered me full time for the winter, good, steady money and I didn't have to be in the cold. I took the deal, we shook hands and I was in.

In hindsight I realized a couple of things that day.

1. Kevin had sent me there to watch Matt Avery just to scare me.

2. I had to continue to evolve with my own style as an Artist.

3. I have the opportunity to play for bigger and more diverse crowds.

4. I could continue to make a living playing music.

5. I was invited to be a part of an elite, unusual and sometimes dysfunctional family.

One of the things I remember most about my first trip to *Kevin's* was one of the bar staff asked me, "What kind of music are you going to play?" I replied, *I am going to play Country Music.* He laughed and said, "That will never last." Huh, I'm still here after thousands of shows on that stage. That person is long gone. *Who's Laughing Now?* I still only know four or five Jimmy Buffett songs.

I am still good friends with Irish Kevin, we have been through a lot over the years. I have gained a lot of wonderful musician friends who I share the stage with. I have worked with some of the most wonderful people I have ever known; musicians, owners, co-workers and friends. I will always have the utmost respect for them and especially Kevin. He gave me a chance to perform on his stage and become the artist I am today. He also indirectly bought me my first house. Thanks Kev!

Were You Born Under A Rock?

I'm not much to remember specific dates, but I do recall a few. One of the most memorable dates in my life was July 17, 2004. On a sunny afternoon in Helsinki, Finland, I was married.

The church where I was married is called *Temppeliaukio Kirkko*, which is translated to "The Rock Church." That is exactly what it is. A beautiful, uniquely designed *place of worship* created inside a giant rock. It is truly an architectural masterpiece and very famous in Finland. On any given day you can see busloads of tourists coming to visit and take pictures of this one-of-a-kind church.

I was married in Finland because that is where my wife is from. The only person in my family that knew I was getting married was my sister, Cindy. The thought of getting my family and friends halfway around the world for my wedding was enormous and expensive. It was just too overwhelming and I decided to keep it secret until afterward. Even my own mother didn't know. It was kind of like we eloped in half.

During the wedding ceremony, the church was full on the left side with all of my wife's friends and family. My side of the church had three people. My best man, Mick was on the altar with me, while his girlfriend, Rita and one of my best friends, Linus were in the pews. That was it, three people on my side. To be honest it looked pathetic, but *it was what it was* and everyone understood why.

On the morning of the wedding, very different from usual wedding traditions, the wife and I woke up and had *mimosas* with my best man and his girlfriend at our apartment. Yes, we saw each other before the wedding. Mick and

I left and went to a hotel just down the street while Marika continued with her preparations for the day.

We bought walkie-talkies and communicated back and forth all afternoon making sure everything was taken care of. One of the exact transmissions I remember went like this,

Me - *How's* it going?

She - "Going well, wine is open."

Me - *Whiskey is open here too.*

We had been out drinking the night before and we needed a *Hair of the dog*, but soon it was also a day for celebration. A few hours later, after a radio check that we were all on time, Mick and I left ten minutes early to walk to the church which was a few blocks away. We timed it out so that we did not see each other before the ceremony in our wedding attire. I had seen her dress prior. It was a white, handmade wedding dress made for her by a woman she knew when she lived in South Africa. I wore a full black suit, black shirt and black shoes. I looked like Johnny Cash.

Mick and I arrived at the church office on schedule as planned.

The minister asked, "Are you ready?" and I replied, *Almost.* I reached in a bag I had brought with me and pulled out my *American Flag Chuck Taylor Converse* shoes and put them on. It had been a tradition for years with all of my best friends back home. Every time someone got married, the groom and groomsmen wore *Chuck Taylors.* I was the last one to get married. Even though my friends were not there, I carried on the tradition. My sister had shipped my shoes to me weeks earlier without my future wife knowing. When we agreed to get married, she said she wanted to be married in Finland. I agreed, but there was no way I was going to go down without a fight. I wanted to make sure that even though I was being married in Finland, there was no misunderstanding that I am American.

I put my black dress shoes under the chair as the minister said to me, "It's time." He looked at me and said, "Aren't you going to change your shoes?" I replied, *I just did.*

Mick and I followed the minister down the hallway to the altar. The minister walked out and said, "Wait here till I give you the sign to come out." I was not nervous at all, as a matter of fact, Mick was more nervous than I was. He was sweaty and visibly pale, also hungover. I was calm and cool and waited in *the wings* just ready to walk out on the altar. To me it was just like waiting to walk out on stage in front of an audience. *I had done this kind of thing a thousand times before, I was ready.*

When the minister was ready, he turned and looked at us for the signal to enter. Still not visible to the congregation, I turned to Mick and said, *Tell me I'm doing the right thing?* His reply was priceless, truly in Mick's Irish style, he just looked at me and said, "You're fucking asking me? I've been divorced twice." Then he shoved me out on the altar in front of the congregation. Those were his brilliant *last words* of encouragement.

We took our place and the music began to reveal my lovely bride entering the back of the church with her father. They were both smiling widely when she looked at me and noticed my shoes. She had no idea I was doing this. Her head dropped and her father leaned over to say something in her ear. I later found out he said, "What is he wearing on his feet?" She replied, "His American flag shoes." He replied, "He is yours."

She arrived at the altar and the ceremony began. It went off without a hitch except for a brief moment. In the middle of a quiet ceremony, from behind me, I heard a little sound and smelled a foul odor. I knew exactly what it was. Mick had farted during the wedding. The man has the worst gas I have ever smelled in my life and he had been drinking *Guinness* the night before. In his nervousness, he *let one go*. He farted in the middle of my wedding! When I turned and looked at him, in true Mick Style, he just smiled innocently and pointed at The Cross in front of us. He blamed the fart on Jesus.

The ceremony ended and we walked down the aisle hand in hand to her packed side of the church. The deal was done. *Dead Man Walking.*

We exited the church to the traditional throwing of the rice and tour buses of tourists who were waiting to get inside to see the church. We departed in the back of a Volkswagen GTI to the sounds of Elvis' *I Can't Help Falling in Love With You*. We stopped, took brief wedding pictures and headed to the nearby reception.

Outside the reception I called my mother to tell her the news. The conversation went like this:

Me - *Mom, I thought you might want to know, I just got married.*

Mom - "Are you drunk?"

Me - *A little, but that›s not why.*

Mom - "Is she pregnant?"

Me - *No.*

I told Mom that I loved her and I would call back later. Yes, it was kind of selfish to get married without telling my own mother, but my mother has never been to Europe and doesn't even have a passport. The logistics would have just been a nightmare. This was for the best for everyone. I promised her we would have a wedding reception in America when we returned and we did, complete with my mother, my family and my closest friends.

The last thing we did before entering the room of the reception was Marika and I both put in our fake, redneck teeth and walked into the room full of her family and friends. Our first photos at the reception look like something out of the movie *Deliverance*. They all knew we were meant to be together and the marriage was off to an interesting future.

I occasionally tell her that we are not really married, because weddings in Finland are not legally recognized in the United States. She still hates that and just tells me to "Shut up."

Nowadays when someone asks me if I was born under a rock? I simply reply, *No, but I was married under one.*

If you ever travel to Helsinki, Finland, go see *The Rock Church*, *Temppeliaukio Kirkko*. It is truly a beautiful place, or as I refer to it *The Scene of the Crime*.

One more date that I remember specifically is May 27, 2007. That was the birth of our son also in Helsinki.

Cock And Balls

When I married my lovely wife in July of 2004 we decided to take our honeymoon in Greece. I had always wanted to go there and it was on my bucket list. We booked a romantic week in Hania on the Greek island of Crete to celebrate. It was beautiful. Neither of us had ever been there before and we loved it. I would love to go back there anytime. We spent a wonderful week in the sun and beauty of the island and took in the Greek Culture. There are few places I have visited that I would like to return to again; Las Vegas, New York, Italy, St Thomas and Greece.

My wife and I had different ideas of how we would spend our vacations. She is very planned, almost to an OCD level. If we go somewhere she has never been, she wants to know as much about that place as she can before arrival. She studies books and tourist literature for weeks or months before our arrival. She wants to know all the tourist sites to see and all about the history, culture, food, transportation and everything. Every moment of every day from the time we wake up until the time we go to bed is taken up with schedules and plans. We travel all over the place all day, walking and exploring. It wasn't a bad thing, we learned and saw a lot, but I usually came back from a vacation just as tired or more so than when I left.

My idea of a vacation is blowing into town, lying on the beach or by the pool, taking a nap or reading a book under a sun umbrella while every once in a while a waitress comes by, shakes my toe to wake me and asked if I would like another drink. I enjoy relaxing, the quiet and peaceful tranquility of the fact that no one knows me or wants me to sing. I enjoy bubble baths, massages; glasses of local red wine and fresh bread with cheese on the balcony of my hotel, taking in the scenery. I like it peaceful and unplanned, just make it up as you go.

We usually went along with my wife's plans. I am okay with that because I am a big fan of History myself. I've loved learning new things, countries, cultures, history and traditions, so we usually booked a guided tour or two and made the best of it.

On our second day in Greece we decided to rent a scooter and set off from the city of Hania to explore the island and see some other small towns in Greek countryside and experience the culture. We took off, headed towards the mountains, with her on the back of the scooter. The scenery was beautiful, we breezed along the backcountry mountain roads twisting and turning through the mountains along the way. I drove mountain roads that had steep, blind curves with no guardrail protecting you from the deep-drop off cliff that was along the edge. I navigated narrow roads with occasionally oncoming traffic and a drop-off into certain death. At times I would come around a blind curve and wind up face-to-face with a goat standing in the middle of the road for no reason. I would slam on the brakes and make my way past. It happened more than once.

We continued through the winding roads, breathtaking views of the big Greek sky and the rolling hills of houses, farms and olive groves below. After a while we decided to stop at a local Greek restaurant, the only one around at the top of a hill overlooking the valley. It was truly a *Greek Restaurant*. The real thing - it had nothing touristy about it and we were going to have an authentic Greek lunch. There were chickens in the dirt parking lot and a few goats as we parked the scooter and headed inside.

We were taken to a lovely table, handed a menu and we began to have a one-of-a-kind dining experience. As I mentioned, we were deep in the Greek countryside and of course the menu was in Greek. No English! Neither one of us could read or speak Greek except *Thank You* and *Hello*. We tried to communicate with the waiter, but it didn't work, we were on our own.

A touch of panic set in, I am NOT an adventurous eater and I don't like trying new foods. I eat the same thing over and over. I am a boring eater. I don't like seafood, I am a meat and potatoes man, and I like to know exactly what I'm eating. I have ordered things abroad before in a different language and what I got to eat was totally different from what I thought I ordered. It was dangerous, terrible and had given me diarrhea in the past. I DON'T like experimenting with my food. I want to know what it is and now it's in Greek? Through the broken language barrier, I made out the word *cock* and a red flag went off in my head. Now I know through the language barrier that *cock* means chicken, but it's still weird to order out loud. I know what they meant, and it's hard to fuck up a chicken. It was the only thing I could identify and I was about to order a plate full of *cock*. As a heterosexual man it just felt unnatural and weird, but it was the only choice I had and I was uncomfortable already.

I ordered *The Cock* and somehow through broken Greek, I believe I was told, it was the *House Specialty*, a local chicken who had been raised, killed fresh and cooked right here at the same spot.

Over a glass of red Greek wine our meal finally arrived. I believe Marika had a salad. On my plate were half a cooked chicken and some vegetables. *Okay, this looks familiar, I can do this,* I said to myself. I am going to try and enjoy this meal and the memory. After eating a bit, I flipped the chicken over and noticed there was something underneath that appeared to be like small onions. What look like small, cooked onions about the size of a quarter, had been invisible from the other side of the chicken. I am not much for onions really, so I'd lightly tap them with my fork to push them away from the chicken. To my surprise the onions snapped right back. I hit them again with my fork and the same thing happened. They would not move, they were somehow attached to the chicken. It was then that I realized that these small, cooked onion-looking things were the balls still attached to the chicken. In some countries this can be a delicacy. Fine! I have no desire to put balls of any kind from any animal or human in my mouth. I got my wife's attention and I said, *Look* as I flicked the fork again. She replied, "Are those onions? Just push them away." I let her know that they could not be removed. They were still attached to the chicken and they were the chicken's testicles. We both looked in horror and disbelief. I had lost my appetite at this point and pushed the plate away. I knew in my head not to order *The Cock* and did it anyway. *Game over!*

We paid the bill and I left half of my chicken complete with the balls untouched. We climbed back on the scooter and whizzed down the mountain through the olive groves laughing about the whole thing. We still laugh about that story today.

In hindsight, it did teach me a few things that I still remember. Anytime I see half a roasted chicken, I always check to see if the balls are still attached. I have to take a look. Also, if I see a roasted chicken it brings back the memory of that day. That chicken changed me forever. He was *well hung* for a chicken, but the most important lesson I learned that day was *DON'T EVER ORDER THE COCK!*

Thanksgiving In Denmark

In November of 2006, I spent the whole month working on a cruise ship from Esbjerg, Denmark to Harwich, England. My wife was pregnant with our son at the time and I spent every day going back and forth across the North Sea.

I was very homesick to say the least, and crossing the sea at that time of year can be very rough. I played every night and watched the waves crash over the bow of the ship onto the windows in front of me on stage. It was like a scene from the movie *The Perfect Storm*. I have played a lot of ships in the past, but I have never been on one that was rougher than that one. They showed *The Poseidon Adventure* every night on the TV. After a few days I started to watch it like it was a documentary to figure out how to escape the boat if needed. It goes without saying there are some movies you should never play on a cruise ship. *The Poseidon Adventure, Titanic*, etc. You should also never show *Snakes on a Plane* when flying. I guess some people just have a sick, twisted sense of humor.

I had all the cabinet doors in my cabin tied shut because things would fly across the room when the boat took a hard roll. I kept the TV on the floor because it would occasionally crash off the shelf. The boat was small to begin with and most of the passengers were not in a party mood, they were just trying to get done with the overnight crossing. I couldn't even stand on the stage. The seas were so rough I had to sit, even with my seasoned *sea legs,* sometimes the boat would catch me off-guard. I was afraid of falling and breaking my guitar or me. A few times the boat moved so hard my stool slipped away from the microphone in the middle of a song. Shortly after, the boat would move again and I would slide back to my original spot like a yo-yo.

I remember many times during that month, going through the hallways of the ship at night, I would feel the boat head up the front of a big wave, I would run as far as I could up the hallway, then when I felt us hit the crest of the wave, I would stop and place both hands on opposing walls to wait for the impending crash. It was like playing a virtual game of the old video game *Frogger*, only this time it was for real. The boat constantly rocked in all directions. I held on to the edge of my bunk to keep from rolling out of bed at night. I learned that one the hard way.

The weather was gray, rainy, windy and cold. It was overall a depressing, dreary month. The only ray of sunshine I had was in a port in Denmark. I had a bag of pot I hid under a rock near a park just outside the harbor. I would get off the ship, go roll a joint and spend the next hours walking up and down the little *Walking Street* in the center of town before heading back to the boat.

I was lonely. I missed my pregnant wife and friends. I was looking forward to the end of the month when Thanksgiving rolled around, but it was the first and only Thanksgiving I ever spent alone.

In years past when I lived in Nashville, I always threw a Thanksgiving party with my roommate, Temple, that we called *Thanksgiving for Misfits*. We and a bunch of our other friends, did not have family in Nashville, so when Thanksgiving came around we all gathered at my house for a big feast and we were each other's family. It was a great tradition, and I think about those Thanksgivings every year.

Thanksgiving is an American holiday, in Europe they do not celebrate it. So to everyone around me it was just Thursday. No one realized it was an important day to me and no one ever said a word. In my gloom I walked down *The Walking Street* looking for any restaurant that might have turkey or something familiar. I found nothing, just a shawarma place and one Thai restaurant. I was really down when I saw the magic arches of *McDonald's*. I figured what the hell? I miss home, and might as well eat some good old-fashioned American food. I stepped up to the counter and ordered a large Quarter Pounder meal, two additional cheeseburgers, an apple pie and a hot fudge sundae. I ate till I was sick. At least that made me feel like Thanksgiving at home, bloated and sleepy. After I stuffed myself, I waddled back to the boat and proceeded to take a nap in a food-induced coma. The people who worked at McDonald's must have thought that I was ordering for a family. Much to their amazement, I ate it all. Not the best Thanksgiving meal I ever had, but I made do with the options available. I had never eaten that much McDonald's in one sitting and haven't since.

The only positive thing that did come out of that month was a little rocking elephant I saw in a toy store window on *The Walking Street*. I'd seen rocking horses for kids before, but never saw a rocking elephant. I bought it for my son on site for his first present, even though he wasn't even born yet. I had it shipped to the United States and we named the elephant *Denmark*. He still has it.

The Ring

For years people have noticed that I wear several rings on my hands, six to be exact, three on my right hand and three on my left hand. I don't do it to be gaudy or boast of wealth, I wear them because each ring means something very personal to me and I just happened to like gold. The obvious ring is the large gold band I wear on my left hand that is my wedding ring. This ring was made by a Finnish designer named Kalevila and is thick and heavy. I love it. You can see it from a long-distance so people know without a doubt I am taken.

The large tiger eye ring on my right ring finger was my father's ring. I remember that ring on his hand my whole life and after his passing, since I am the oldest son, I now take the lead male role in the family. I take this ring very seriously. To me it was like passing down the crown and throne to the next in line of royalty.

On my right index finger I wear a ring that my wife bought for me on our honeymoon in Greece. It is engraved with a circle that represents long life. On my right thumb I wear a simple gold band that I purchased on my first trip to Estonia. To me it represents an American being in the former Soviet Union and the changing of times in the world. On my left little finger I actually wear two rings. Both simple gold bands. The first one was given to me many years ago as a Christmas gift from my sister. She bought it for me when she traveled to the Caribbean. It was the first ring I ever received and I had worn it ever since for more than twenty five years. The last ring I wear is the one that is significant but still a mystery.

One night while working on a ship, after the show, I returned to my cabin to count my tip jar from the evening. Among the bills and mass of foreign coins at the bottom was a simple gold band. I immediately realized someone had inadvertently dropped the ring into my tip jar and lost it. I called the front desk and informed them that if they had anyone reporting a lost ring, I have it and they can gladly have it back.

Days went by and no one ever said a word about the ring again. I placed the small ring on my little finger and left the ship a few weeks later.

When I returned home I showed the ring to my wife and told her the story of how I found it. She explained that it is a Finnish engagement ring.

Different countries and cultures have varied traditions when it comes to getting engaged. In Finland when a couple gets engaged, the woman receives a simple band to wear on her left hand and so does the man. No big, gaudy, expensive, 10 carat blue diamond like in the States. Just a simple, plain band is enough. It's very subtle, but a very nice tradition. My wife explained to me the tradition of the Finish engagement rings and asked me if I had looked on the inside of the ring? I never thought to look for an engraving, besides, the ring looked more like a small wedding band to me rather than an engagement ring. I pulled it off my finger and she looked on the inside. There engraved in small print, it said, *Mia 7/1985*. It was a man's engagement ring. Several questions came to mind at this point.

1. How big was this dude? This ring is small and only fits on my little finger. If he wore this on his ring finger he must have been tiny.

2. Why was it in my tip jar?

3. Was there a couple at my show who had had a fight and in the heat of the argument he threw the ring in my tip jar?

4. Maybe he had carried this ring for a long time in memory of a loved lost and now just decided it was time to move on?

5. Maybe the girl had it and just decided to let it go?

6. Maybe they broke up at my show?

7. Maybe it was at the bottom of the change-pocket on someone's wallet and they accidentally dumped it into my tip jar with the

other coins? (That happens with a lot of people trying to get rid of small foreign coins.)

The scenarios and questions are endless, but I still have no answer to how or why I got this ring?

Till this day I wear this ring on the chance that someday I might meet the owner and they can have the ring back if they want it. I never know what is going to happen in my unpredictable life, and stranger things have happened.

I still wonder what the story was behind this mysterious ring. However, I know one thing for certain, apparently, I have been engaged to a girl named Mia since August of 1985. If I ever meet her, I hope she is smoking hot! With my luck she won't be.

Stalkers And Fans

I learned early in my career some very valuable rules.

1. DON'T use your real name.

2. Do not have your name and address listed in the phone book.

3. Nowadays, don't give *just anyone* your cell phone number

I had my first Fan/Stalker experience when I was in college as the morning producer at a local radio station in Pittsburgh. Up to this time I used my real last name. No, Harris is not my real last name.

One year we had a Valentine's contest live on the air, kind of like *The Dating Game*. Three eligible bachelors questioned by a bachelorette and vice versa. We did the promotion as usual and the "winning couples" received one night on the town, with dinner, a few bars and a limo along with the morning DJ. He was uneasy about going out with the contest winners and asked me to join him in case of any trouble.

As the night went along and more drinks were had by the contestants, the *female winner* decided she was more interested in me than her *prize-winning man*. Awkward! I am working here. At the end of the night we all returned to the radio station and went our separate ways. For a few weeks after that, the *female winner* (let's just call her that) showed up at the radio station early in the morning when we were on the air. I'm talking early, 6 a.m. before the offices would open. I could see her standing outside the glass door, hovering in the hallway of the high rise building we were in, waiting for a chance to talk to me and looking like a cat about to pounce on a mouse. *Houston we have a problem.* Thank God for door locks.

She also called my home phone (yes, at that time I was in the phone book). One time she even showed up at my apartment and rang the doorbell. When I opened the door, I let out an audible scream then slammed the door. She showed up outside after my college classes, trying to catch me on my way back to the radio station. I was beginning to feel a little freaked out. I was being stalked.

The final straw, as I left work one evening and walked out of the office building, she was lurking on the sidewalk waiting for me. I ran across the river bridge in a full sprint from downtown Pittsburgh to the parking lot of *Three Rivers Stadium* where I left my car. (Probably the last time I ran in my life.) Much to my surprise, when I finally got to my car, there was a love note underneath my windshield wiper. There were thousands of cars that parked there every day and this crazy bitch searched through them all until she found mine. That bitch was nuts! I moved to a different address shortly after that, got an unlisted number, and I no longer used my real last name.

I had another lady that would call me when I worked overnight shifts on the radio in Nashville. She would call the request line, and of course, I would answer. She would say, "Hello Jeff, play *Misty* for me." (Ever see the Clint Eastwood movie?) It's every DJ's worst nightmare. I still hate that movie. Then she would proceed to tell me she was sitting in the parking lot waiting till I got off the air. She wanted to take me to breakfast. Thank God for locked doors and secure parking garages. I always snuck out the back.

Things really took a step up when I started playing music full time. Let me say there are *Fans* and there are *Stalkers*. Stalkers sometimes say "I am your number one fan." (*Misery* by Stephen King.) Yes, I have one of those till this day. I will just say this, I am, in a way, flattered by the fact that they are deeply moved by me and my music. However, sometimes I am scared shitless of what they might do? (Ever see the movie *Selena*?) They just have that crazy *Glenn Close Look* in their eyes. My friend and longtime radio buddy, Rick Marino, coined a phrase "She's a Bunny Boiler." Get the point?

So back to my *Number One Fan* - this woman freaks me out. That entire movie freaks me out as well and I like my ankles. I will just say she is from one of the New England states and comes to see my show several times a year. I never know when or where. She just walks into a show with a big smile on her face and says, "Here I am, your number one fan" and opens her arms for a hug. At this point, I am in sheer panic inside. My experience kicks in. I just smile and quickly throw out a hand for a shake and say, *Good to see you again.* I try to keep her at arm's distance because I never know if she's going to hug me or stab me? So far, so good. It is still unnerving every time.

I was playing a show on a cruise ship in Sweden when I invited a lovely sixtyish lady on stage to serenade her. Now in my defense, I have done this trick for years and it always goes over well. The lady happened to be sitting with a few other couples, and I assumed they were all married and out for a little weekend trip. How do I know? I don't know them?

I did the song *Always on my Mind* then she sat back down and I continued my show. Very simple and innocent. At the end of my show I packed up my guitar and was headed for my room. That is when the sixtyish woman returned to talk to me. She asked if I would like to come have a drink with her? I replied, *Thank you, but I am tired and headed for bed.* I asked her where her friends and husband were? She replied she was not with them, she was on the trip alone. Uh-oh! I politely excused myself and headed for my cabin.

I showered, changed clothes and decided to go get something to eat in the *Crew Mess* before bed. Upon opening the secure crew area door to the passenger hallway, I spotted her lurking outside, waiting to see if I would reappear. She had followed me to my cabin's hallway without me knowing. She could not get into my hallway because of the electronic locks. I opened the door and then immediately slammed it shut in fear. *Shit I am trapped!* I managed to sneak out another crew door to the outside deck and make my way for a snack before returning to my cabin without being caught. For TWO years after that, anytime I would play those ships, she would show up unannounced. I would just walk in the room getting ready to play and there she was in the front row. My stomach dropped every time. I knew I was going to have to deal with her for the next two nights.

On one cruise she had told everyone at the show that I was her boyfriend. *False!* She knew I was married. She left me love letters at the front desk. She sent emails to my website. She asked me to send her a postcard from my honeymoon. She actually asked me to write songs about her and her cats. I was invited to come stay with her at her house in Sweden and she would cook for me anytime. (Remember *Misery*.) She even bought a present for my unborn son, a little stuffed tiger face. (I threw it away.) I was afraid there was a hidden camera in it.

The last time I saw her, she showed up in the front row at a show wearing a short mini skirt. She obviously had a lot of wine before I arrived. While I was singing, anytime I looked in her direction, she would uncross her legs and change positions, revealing what lay underneath. (The old *Sharon Stone Move!*) It was horrible! I have never looked at a ceiling more during a show than I did that night. After that night I never saw her again. I wished her well and said goodbye. I stopped doing the serenade trick in Europe after that.

One time in Key West, a lady in her mid-forties approached me at the front of the stage just before I started my show. I walked over to address her, because she REALLY wanted to speak with me. I immediately realized she had obviously been partaking in *Key West Fun* and had a few cocktails. She proceeded to tell me that she and her husband had seen me a few years earlier and decided to come back to Key West to see my show again. They drove for two days. I was so flattered. They traveled all that way, paid a lot of money and the only reason was to see me perform live in person. I gushed, and so did she. At the exact same moment she spewed projectile vomit all over the stage at my feet. Great way to start off a show. *Clean-up on Aisle Six!*

Her husband took her out. She never did see my show.

The Best Shows I Ever Played.

Sometimes the crowd is just not as big as you would like it to be. I have done many shows over the years to just a handful of people. Sometimes the bar patrons are just nonexistent. Maybe the weather is beautiful and no one wants to be inside? They would rather be out in the fresh air? Sometimes I play on a slow week or holiday. Weekdays are always different from Friday or Saturday nights. Sometimes it's just the slow season and people are elsewhere. It's okay. It happens and I have learned not to take it personally.

When you're a *Big Rockstar* doing arenas for *Big Money,* advertised as *One Night Only* shows and no one shows up, then you can worry. When you play almost three hundred shows a year like I do, it happens, it's just the law of averages.

I personally don't care if the crowd is ten people or ten thousand. It makes no difference to me and what I do. It does not change my personality. They get the same effort, professionalism and respect either way. They could easily go somewhere else to watch live music, but they chose to come see me, and I am grateful. Large crowds are great, you can easily feed off their energy and get lost in the music and the show.

I actually enjoy the slower shows more. It gives a much more intimate feel from me and I get a chance to chat with the audience and get to know them. I feel more relaxed with less pressure and I get to be more of an artist than *A Dancing Monkey* with a guitar. On slower shows I get to play songs that I don't usually play in the busy shows. I show the audience my versatility and true style as an Artist. There are times I have made just as much money in tips and sold more CD's on a slow show than I would have in a packed house. It's the *nature of the beast.* It's always a crapshoot. However, I enjoy what I do and you take the good with the bad.

Yes, I have played shows to an empty room. I have played shows to only one person who did or didn't listen, but I still played on. The best shows I ever played started in 2007.

In May of 2007 I became a father. My wife, newborn son and I moved to Key West and I began to finally work full time at *Irish Kevin's.* For years I'd been working the winter season in Key West and toured Europe or the States for the rest of the year. I was on the road a lot.

My wife wanted to be a stay-at-home mom and I respected that. I began to play five nights a week locally and stopped traveling so I could be at home every night with my family. I am glad I made that decision.

When Elvis was still a baby (Yes, that is a nickname we gave him before he was born) I would sit and play guitar and sing to him in the afternoon. He would smile and laugh. His big eyes would stare at me in the amazement of the sounds I made. When he got a little older he would clap his hands, dance and try to sing along. They were truly the best shows I've ever played and they were to an audience of one. The look of that big toothless grin is something I will *Always* remember.

The Concert Series continued for years. A few years later he began to go to preschool. I was surprised when he asked me one day if I had a job? All of his friends' fathers had jobs, but I was always at home. He thought I didn't have a job. In his defense it was a legitimate question. Every night Mommy and I would give him a bath, feed him and put him to bed. What he didn't see was after that, Daddy would make a pot of coffee, get a shower, put on stage clothes and go to work. I would come home in the middle of the night and go to bed before he woke up. He never knew I was gone. He thought I was home all of the time. Yes, my job is far from a normal nine-to-five job like his friends' fathers, but I do have a job and I explained to him what I did. He replied to me, "And they pay you money to do that?" I laughed and said, *Yeah buddy, that's my job. But remember the most important job I have in the world is to be your daddy.* It still is.

One of my proudest moments in life came about a year later. He was still in preschool and the teacher asked a family questionnaire. She wanted to know what his daddy's job was? He answered, *"Rockstar."* Still one of my proudest moments, although it's far from the truth, that is what I was to him in his eyes. I laughed and gushed as I read his response. Mommy wasn't very impressed when his answer about her was, "She is just mommy." Silly kids.

I miss those afternoon concerts upstairs in the bedroom of our little townhouse, but they grow up fast. We still have our afternoon *Jam Sessions*, except nowadays he plays drums along with me. Music is in his genes as well. He is truly talented, he has great rhythm, sings on pitch and even writes his own material. I am very proud!

Being a father is the best thing I have ever done in my life. Better than any song, book or poem I've ever written. More precious than any money I have ever made from this crazy musical career. The real *Rockstar* is him. In many ways he is a lot like me, but I hope he does not decide to do what I do for a living. I would not wish some of the things I have seen or done on my worst enemies. The Music Business is a tough, dirty business and I hope he chooses a different path in his life. I don't push him to play music, sing or perform. I let him enjoy it at his own pace and free will. When he was small he used to come onstage with me from time to time, but now he gets a little freaked out by the drunken strangers who want to talk to him after he gets off stage. I can't blame him, so do I.

Although I love our *Jam Sessions*, I hope he takes another direction in his personal journey later in life. Only time will tell?

One thing is for sure, I will be there to support him either way.

Simple Things

Simple things in life make me happy. A hug and a smile from my son, a good pizza and a morning cup of coffee on my front porch in my rocking chair.

I've spent a large majority of my life being a *Night Person*; hating mornings mostly because I was up late due to my profession. As I get older I find mornings to be more wonderful. The chance to breathe the fresh air, listen to the silence or the song of the birds and reboot your soul before the reality of the day sets in. I do a lot of my writing in the morning. As a matter of fact, I'm currently writing this about 7 a.m. Yes, I said 7 in the morning. I get the chance to think about my life and what I want to share while my mind is still fresh. It's absolutely wonderful. Watching the sun come up on a brand-new day while thinking about what message I want to pass on to the world.

I have also found that a lot of my fellow musician friends are now turning into the same way I am. We've spent most of our lives like musical vampires; when the sun came up we went to bed. After all these years, (maybe it's age?) we are all beginning to see things in a different light. It's a good thing. It's hard to see the beauty of life in the dark.

I hope someday you get to experience it as well - the peaceful calm of the world before all the daily hell breaks loose.

Things You Don't Know About Me

My favorite color is blue, but I am partial to green because it's the color of money, but I hate green *Stage Lights* they make you look ill.

I learned to play guitar at the age of eighteen.

I have worked as a strawberry picker, a paperboy, an ice cream shop attendant, was a cook in a steakhouse, delivered pizzas, was a construction worker, a real estate agent, stagehand, bartender, radio DJ, strip club DJ and a musician.

I love the sound of church bells, rain on a tin roof and train whistles.

My favorite song is *Same Old Lang Syne* by Dan Fogelberg. (I don't play it.)

I don't like the smell or taste of seafood and I live on an island.

I hate snakes and pretty much all reptiles. I find them creepy and gross. I don't even like to look at them.

My favorite place I've ever traveled to is the island of Crete in Greece.

I hate to see a woman cry.

I enjoy my quiet time away from crowds. I would rather go to a nice, quiet, dark dinner and have a glass of wine than be in a big, loud and rowdy bar.

The best thing I've ever done is become a father.

My favorite food is pizza. I also love bacon, ice cream, coffee and peanut butter.

My favorite movie is *Blazing Saddles*.

My favorite singer is George Jones.

My Favorite Quotes

Here are some of the favorite quotes I have heard over the years. I will not use real names to protect the innocent.

"Don't just think you're going to blow into town, fuck me in the ass then not talk to me anymore."

"That looks like socks on a chicken."

"I had never kissed a girl with an Adam's Apple before."

"You might want to stretch out, this is going to hurt."

"I feel like I was raped by a tribe of pygmies."

"You hit me? Really? You hit me?"

"It's okay to sleep with her, she's my wife."

"Someone shit my pants last night."

"When you're on stage, don't talk to the audience. Talk to the people outside, walking down the street, they're more important."

"Does this look infected to you?"

"Are you into fitness? How about fitness in your mouth." JMH

"Why don't you give me some of that good pussy? I know you have it on you."

"Burning is normal when you pee, right?"

"Someone call the coroner; his career is dead."

"Two twenty-one year-old girls at the same time equals one forty-two year-old girl."

"Did we have sex last night? If we did, I apologize."

"I just found out you can't refinance your home if you rent."

"If breathing required brains, she would be dead."

"She has a face for radio."

"How much do you weigh? I want to make sure I can eat all of you."

"I would take three little blue pills for her."

"Never underestimate the stupidity of people in crowds."

"He can drink a 2 into a 10."

"Sometimes you just get tired of fucking people in the alley."

"The next time I 'play choke you', I ain't playing."

"I am going to fuck you so hard tonight when you're asleep."

"I'm going to come down there and kick you right in the pussy." (Okay, that one was me.)

"Sure, you can fuck me in the ass, but you can't take me to dinner?"

"There's always time for pussy!"

Written By Jeff Harris
© 2020